DARK, NO SUGAR

BY WARREN LEIGHT

★

★

DRAMATISTS
PLAY SERVICE
INC.

2

MR. MORTON WAITS FOR HIS BUS
was originally produced at the Ensemble Studio Theater
as part of the Marathon 2005: The Original Festival of One-Act Plays.

THE FINAL INTERROGATION OF CEAUSESCU'S DOG
was originally produced at The Ensemble Studio Theater
as part of the Marathon 2000: The Original Festival of One-Act Plays.

AMICI, ASCOLTATE was originally produced at
The Duke on 42nd Street as part of
Armed & Naked in America: A Naked Angels Issues Project.

SPECIAL NOTE ON SONGS AND RECORDINGS

For performances of copyrighted songs, arrangements or recordings mentioned in these Plays, the permission of the copyright owner(s) must be obtained. Other songs, arrangements or recordings may be substituted provided permission from the copyright owner(s) of such songs, arrangements or recordings is obtained; or songs, arrangements or recordings in the public domain may be substituted.

CONTENTS

THE FINAL
INTERROGATION OF
CEAUSESCU'S DOG

CHARACTERS

THE INTERROGATOR — A pencil-pushing bureaucrat.

CEAUSESCU'S DOG — A loyal, devoted friend waiting patiently for his master's return.

PLACE

Bucharest.

TIME

New Year's Eve, 1989.

THE FINAL INTERROGATION OF CEAUSESCU'S DOG

A small interrogation room. A man paces, smokes cigarettes. A dog sits on a chair. The man is thin and exhausted. He wears a threadbare winter coat. The dog displays a regal bearing and wears a warmer coat. Both speak in a Rumanian accent, but the dog's accent is of a higher class. Throughout the interrogation, the dog very seldom makes eye contact with the man, and never loses his composure.

MAN. The people believe you are beyond reform. Some want you to suffer; others, to die right away. Because ours is now a just and fair system, you are entitled to make a statement. What do you have to say for yourself?

DOG. I am Ceaucescu's dog. His daughter's dog, actually, but she is rather unstable. Even though he gave me to her, I have always considered him to be my true master.

MAN. You know that your master was a cruel and ruthless tyrant who brought misery to his people and shame to his nation?

DOG. I am dog of Ceaucescu, and my relationship to him is simple relationship of dog to master.

MAN. You do acknowledge that master was a tyrant?

DOG. No. The wife can be a bit stern, I will say that. And the daughter, as I say, has many moods. But I am my master's pride and joy and I've known nothing but love and affection from him.

MAN. You are talking about the most reviled despot in our nation's history. Do you understand that anyone still loyal to him is subject to the death penalty?

DOG. Listen, where is my master? He will straighten this whole thing out, and you will be sorry. Let me tell you.

MAN. Your master is dead. He was shot … like a dog. In the courtyard, as he tried to flee the people's wrath on Christmas Day.

DOG. He will not be happy when he hears how you have treated me.

MAN. He is not coming back. He has gone straight to hell, where he will burn for all time.

DOG. He travels often, you know. Just last month he was in Iran. They love him everywhere he goes. He told me so.

MAN. He was shot dead. He is not coming back.

DOG. I see.

MAN. Do you?

DOG. No. I am simple dog.

MAN. The people believe you are beyond reform.

DOG. I am simple doggie.

MAN. But you lived on imported meat. While our people were starving, you ate the finest veal.

DOG. Sometimes lamb or steak.

MAN. While people starved.

DOG. I did not see any people starving.

MAN. You didn't?

DOG. The people at the palace were all well fed. They ate anything I left over. Often they even pinched some for themselves — but what can you do — servants.

MAN. I have heard they weighed your veal on a scale of gold.

DOG. Yes, and I will tell you the truth, that was not done for my benefit. The gold, I always felt, left a slight metallic taste. I believe this all came about so that the servants would not pinch from my supper.

MAN. While our people lacked basic medical care, you were given drugs and vitamins flown in from Prague.

DOG. I have allergies.

MAN. You were bathed daily in glacier water.

DOG. I hated the baths. Again, because of my allergies, I —

MAN. How did you feel about the sacrifices the people were making? The suffering they endured while you were pampered.

DOG. The people always loved me. The servants were especially kind to me. Once ... once, I was mistreated, but that did not happen again.

MAN. Yes, you bit the hand of Salvo, while he was feeding you. He slapped you, and then because he slapped you, he was put to death. Is that correct?

DOG. I was not slapped again by him.

MAN. It's true, then, that you bit the hand that fed you?

DOG. Sure.

MAN. Why?

DOG. *It tastes good.*

MAN. *(Restrains himself.)* Weren't you aware that it might cause suffering?

DOG. I did not suffer.

MAN. But the man whose hand you bit —

DOG. I don't understand.

MAN. You bit the man's hand.

DOG. Yes. Of course.

MAN. He was trying to feed you?

DOG. Yes. Yes. But we've been over this.

MAN. Weren't you aware it might cause suffering?

DOG. I did not suffer.

MAN. But the man whose hand you bit …

DOG. Yes!?

MAN. Did you not, for one second, think about him, his hand, the pain you — *(Dog stares at the man's hand, which is close to the dog's mouth.)*

DOG. His hand was here. If he did not want me to bite it he should not have placed it so near my teeth. Listen, where is my master, he will straighten this out.

MAN. Your master is dead!

DOG. You don't know him.

MAN. *(Very frustrated.)* The interrogation can not end until … *(Calms himself again.)* In your house, you had your own Oriental rug.

DOG. It was Bokhara.

MAN. A Bokhara?

DOG. Yes. Again, this was not my choice. I liked the *feel* of it but its taste was nothing to get excited about.

MAN. *(Outraged.)* And this rug was red, was it not? The same color as the blood shed by our people under the hand of your master?

DOG. Again, I loved the feel of it, but the color, that was for them. I do not see color, you know. I am simple dog.

MAN. You are a simple dog?

DOG. Yes.

MAN. Then fetch. *(He throws his hat on the ground.)*

DOG. Pardon.

MAN. Fetch this, simple doggie. Come on! Fetch little doggie. *(The man now drops to his knees. He lifts the hat up and down, to try to capture the dog's attention. The dog, as always, couldn't care less.)*

DOG. You are joking.

MAN. Jump up. Jump! Go on. Jump. Jump. You are simple dog,

11

then fetch. Fetch. Come on! *(The man seems to have completely lost it now. He is on all fours, by the dog's chair. The dog looks at him with utter disdain.)*

DOG. Are you out of your mind? Do you know who my master is?

MAN. *(Crying now.)* He is not coming back.

DOG. Really, well, in that case, I will just sit right here and wait for him to come back. You may go now. When I want something, I will let you know. *(The man, broken, sits by the dog's chair. The dog seems unmoved. After a while, he disdainfully reaches out to pat the man on the head. Then decides against it, as the lights fade to black.)*

End of Play

PROPERTY LIST

Bureaucrat's hat

MR. MORTON WAITS
FOR HIS BUS

CHARACTERS

OFFICER SHEEHY — A nervous rookie cop.

MR. MORTON — An elderly, elegant corpse.

MR. MORTON WAITS
FOR HIS BUS

*A tenement studio — day. Officer Sheehy (young, thin nerv-
ous rookie cop) on his walkie, on hold, in a studio crammed
with fifty years of an urbane man's life. A huge clay bowl of
prescription pills. Clothes and bathrobes and piles of papers
on chairs. A partially closed convertible sofa.*

SHEEHY. Me again. Still looking for … Oh Sarge, it's Sheehy.
Happy Fourth to you too, Sarge. I got a … I got a … a DOA. *(He
looks at the corpse of Mr. James Morton, an old man, comfortably dead,
in a wing chair. Morton seems elegant even in death, a sheet partially
wraps him.)* An old guy. Top floor, six story walk-up. Yeah, I know: It's
always a six story walk-up. The neighbors called it in. A nice couple
— Tommy and his wife Richard — they had the keys to his place.
   They check in on him every morning cause … you know, he's
old. Yeah — they said heart trouble. Valve, or something. Tom, or
Richard, I don't know — the blond one, in the shorts, found him
on the floor. Must've been trying to make his bed. Although why I
couldn't tell you … you wouldn't believe this place.
   Yeah, it's my first one, but … I can handle it. All I have to do is
sit here until EMS or the morgue sends a bus, right? I mean, how long
will that take? … You're kidding. No, I know it's a holiday weekend,
I'm supposed to see my — no, it's all right. Overtime is good.
   Did I find his what? His address book? *(Spies it on bedside table.)*
Yeah. First thing I looked for. OK, OK. *(Writes down his Sarge's
requests, repeats them back, tries to affect an "it's all routine" tone.)* Try
to get someone to sign off on cause of death. Over the phone will
do? OK? … Yup. Yup. Yes, I have my stickers. *(Checks frantically,
finds "Sealed by order of the police department" sticker.)* Piece of cake.
   ANYTHING ELSE? Keep the A.C. on high. Why? Oh.
   Duh. Voucher the keys. Um, he has a watch. I will. What's
that? What? Oh yeah, course I have. First thing I did. *(Forces him-*

17

self now to check the eyes of the corpse.) THEY'RE … CLOSED. YUP. CLOSED.

Don't worry Sarge, the situation is under control. Thank you, sir. I appreciate your faith in me. *(Hangs up. Sheehy turns, sneaks another look at the closed eyes, and lifeless body of Mr. Morton.)* O. Kayyy. Looks like it's just … the two of us. *(No answer. It's very quiet. Sheehy leans back, exhales. Suddenly, from an offstage bathroom, the toilet flushes.)* Ahh! *(He jumps up and turns around.)* Who's there? *(No one. Goes to the bathroom door. Kicks it open. Hand on his holster. Command voice:)* This is the police. *(He partially enters. Empty. The toilet flushes again. He looks up to an ancient overhead wood tank. To the tank:)* That's enough out of you. *(Backing into the living area, talks to corpse.)* You oughtta get that toilet looked at. *(The phone rings, almost giving Sheehy his second heart attack. To himself:)* It's just the phone. Idiot. … *(The machine picks up. The voice is effete and yet patrician.)*

ANSWERING MACHINE. You've reached the home of James Morton. I am unable to answer the phone right now …

SHEEHY. I'll say.

ANSWERING MACHINE. *(Continuing, almost responding.)* … but if you leave your name, number, and a brief message, I will get back to you. *(The machine beeps.)*

SHEEHY. Wait — could be next of kin. *(Looks around.)* Where's the phone? *(To corpse.)* Phone? … You're a lot of help. Where's the friggen phone? *(Sheehy tries to step over the piles to get to the machine.)*

DEE DEE. *(Voiceover.)* James, it's Dee Dee — are you there?

SHEEHY. I'm coming.

DEE DEE. *(Voiceover.)* James. Pick up.

SHEEHY. Lady — I'm trying. *(He gets to the machine but can't find phone.)*

DEE DEE. *(Voiceover.)* We're waiting for you at Penn Station. *(He picks up a wire coming out of the machine, follows it to the phone. On top of a table behind the couch. Under some clothes.)* We're still hoping you can join us before the fireworks. Lots of love, luv. *(He leans half way over the couch, picks up the phone.)*

SHEEHY. Hello. Hello. *(Too late. To corpse:)* They hung up … *(Looks at phone machine.)* Eight messages. Wow. My old man lives alone. If I don't call him, he can go weeks without talking to someone. You — you've got friends. Don't you. *(No answer.)* Let's call 'em up; find your next of kin. *(From the corpse now, the noise of flatulence.)* You're not … oh God … are you, passing gas? Or? … Oh

Jesus. *(Another bad noise. Longer now.)* Oh Jesus. *(He looks at the sheet that partially wraps Mr. Morton. Gets skeeved out. Bolts up, runs — knocking over a stack or two of books — to the bathroom, off the kitchen. We hear the sound of him retching, then flushing the toilet. Comes out, splashes some water on his face. Dries it off with a skeevy hand towel. To Morton:)* It's disgusting in there … *(To himself.)* Where was I? Next of kin. *(Sheehy goes back to the phone. Picks up phone but now gets distracted by a stack of Playbills next to the phone.)* Look at all these Playbills. What did you do, like go out every night? A real Ladies Man. *(Finds a Helmut Newton photo book, with a beautiful model in bondage on the cover. While Sheehy reads, Morton's eyes slowly drift open, Sheehy doesn't notice.)* Hello! *(Opens it to pics of women in bondage.)* Now we're talking. *(Sees that it's signed. Reading:)* To James, love always, Helmut. Helmut? *(Looks at cover. Looks at photos. Stares at pics of cheesecake. Then more pics of beefcake in bondage. He looks, flips to another page, looks, flips again, looks. Then he realizes he's been looking at pictures of naked men. Closes the book fast.)* Helmut Newton. You know this guy? There's some seriously sick queer shit in here, my friend. I don't know if you want your family to — *(He hides the book under the fold-out couch. Now he turns to the corpse and sees its eyes are open. Sheehy is in shock.)* Ahh! … Mr. Morton. Your eyes. Are you — *(The corpse doesn't react. Dead is dead.)* Hey … why don't you … rest? In peace. *(Sheehy kneels at the corpse's side. He looks at the old man's face. Now he puts on a latex glove and closes the corpse's eyes. Gently. He looks back at the corpse as he starts to get up. Mr. Morton's eyes pop right back to open position.)* Ahh! … *(He takes a breath.)* Come on now. Work with me, Mr. Morton. *(This time he uses his shirt sleeve to close Morton's eyes. As he moves his hand away, a beat passes.)* Where is that bus? It should have been here an hour ago. *(He edges toward a bedside table, which is piled high with tchotkes, ashtrays and packs of cigarettes. Firecrackers go off outside.)* You smoked. That was dumb. Dumb dumb dumb. I used to do it. 'Til my mom got emphysema. Put 'em away right then. Promised her I would, and I did. Just takes will power. I don't even miss 'em. Don't miss 'em at all *(Looks longingly at, then fondles, a pack of Pall Malls. He puts them down and instead picks up a deck of playing cards. Partially clears off a table, sits. Shuffles cards, begins solitaire game.)* This is not how I wanted to spend my Fourth.

My dad, Detective Jack Sheehy, he never had the Fourth off either. But he got parade duty. Or the tall ships. Remember those? '85? '86? He pulled some strings downtown. Got me on this police boat for that. That was something. The tall ships. Yup. *(Decides to level with Morton.)* Actually it was a disaster. I got seasick. Puked all over this one detective. Always had a … sensitive stomach. Guess you saw that. Of course, you're not exactly a model of digestive decorum yourself. Those friggen guys at the Sixth. Everything's a test with them. It's probably all over the station house by now. "Hey, guess what the Sarge got Sheehy doing? He put the string bean on a DOA." And if I call in and say, "Where's my friggen bus?" I'll never hear the end of it. It's all a test. I'm not calling. We just sit tight. You're cool. I'm cool.

The thing is — the whole point of becoming a cop is so that people take you seriously. I mean, not the whole point, there's fighting crime and … serving the community. And so forth. But also, the badge commands respect. Except for when the guys bust my balls.

I missed a couple of days, cause I had, like, this tooth thing. Still do. My wisdom teeth are all … Right away the guys are going: "Hey, rookie, the tooth fairy visit yet?"

"Hey rookie, you pee standing up? Just wondering." C'mon, cut me a — like I don't do my job. *(This reminds him of something. He puts the cards down.)* For example, now would be a good time to voucher your valuables. They'll be here any minute. You're kind of an easy mark right now. *(He kneels at the waist of the corpse, gently picks up Morton's wrist.)* I thought you'd be cooler by now. I guess … this heat.

Here we go — *(He examines the watch.)* Cartier? Very nice, Mr. Morton. *(He lifts the corpse's hand. Tries to get the watch off. As he does so, the rigored hand clasps his, and locks on.)* Mr. Morton, let go. *(He tries to pry open the fingers. Really wrestling now, he manages to pull away, then looks up to see Morton's eyes, WHICH ARE OPEN AGAIN, and staring at him.)* Ahh! *(Sheehy jumps back, tries to stay calm.)* OK, Mr. Morton. *(He looks around, spies his sunglasses on the table. Grabs them, and puts them on Mr. Morton.)* Just try to relax. OK? The bus is coming. *(He edges away.)* The bus is coming. *(Notices.)* Getting dark out there … *(Takes a cigarette now.)* You are what they call low priority, my friend. Old man, lives alone, dies of natural causes. On a three day weekend … It was natural causes, wasn't it. You're not holding out on me, are you? *(No answer. Lights cigarette, inhales.)* It's been a long day. *(As he smokes, he starts to realize his tooth aches.)* Yup, a real long — god this thing is killing me … You have any … aspirin? I got this bad … wisdom tooth. I already told you that, didn't I.

20

Supposed to get it taken out. But — you know, I keep thinking, once it comes in a little, it'll be easier. *(Goes to the bowl. Starts rummaging.)* You got everything else in that pinata bowl. You have to have some Advil or something. Tylenol with codeine? C'mon. C'mon … This tooth is really killing me. Bingo: Percoset. Percodan. Perco-perco- *(Gets giddy, tosses the containers in the air.)* -percodan. Makes me feel like a percoman. *(He takes one, swallows it. Then takes another. Instantly feels better.)* Thank you, Mr. Morton. Oh yeah, thank you. *(He goes back to a game of solitaire.)* Seven on the eight. The perfect mate. Four on a five. We're feeling alive. Jack. Jack? What do I do with a jack? *(Puts the cards down.)* Call him. *(He picks up the phone, dials.)* Hey. Happy Fourth.

It's Jack Jr.

Your son, Little Jack. Just calling in. You know — do I have to have a reason?

Just calling to wish you a happy Fourth.

No I'm not trying to be goddamned funny. I was just thinking of you. You always had to work on the holidays, and now I'm doing it, I don't know if I ever, you know, thanked you, for …

No — I'm on sort of a special assignment. Security …

Hah! Terrorism detail? No. Terrorism? In the Sixth?

No, Dad. I'm not holding out on you. OK you really want to know? I'm just sort of … ah … they put me with a DOA. I'm waiting for the bus. Yeah. I know.

It's been like … seven hours. Yup. Yup. *(Defensive.)* No. I know, take what they give you. And deal with it. That's what got you through. I know. No sir.

Has he started to what? Smell? Well, he — *(Gags after this, tries to cover.)* Not yet, I guess. Just a little rigor — I'm looking right at him. *(He isn't. Sheehy gags more. Covers the phone.)* No. Of course I didn't vomit, Dad. That was a long time ago. OK? I'm a cop now.

I just — look — Dad. I don't need a lecture. I'm doing fine. Yeah, I'm one of the guys.

No one thinks I'm soft. Believe me.

No. Not one partner yet. They shift me a — Dad, it's not me. I got their confidence. There's been, a lot of turnover lately. We're just… short staffed. I'm golden here. So it's all … yeah, no, it's good. And you? *(He flips cards while half-listening.)* Uh hah.

Hmm hhh.

Yuh.

Well go easy on those, Dad. *(Reacts to a bad card.)* Damn it.

21

No, sorry, Dad. The ah — this phone. Friggen old. You wouldn't believe this place. Makes your basement look like a Good Housekeeping Award Winner.

Dad, it's just a joke.

I didn't mean anything by that. It's just a —

Dad? Dad. *(Sheehy realizes dad's hung up on him. He puts the phone down, spies a few decanters of booze, goes to them, pours himself a scotch, downs it.)* He hung up. You believe that. *(Pours himself another.)* One minute you're talking the next minute he's like …

Bet you were a good father. Not a three six-pack a day guy like my old man. *(He looks at some photos of Mr. Morton. Mr. Morton in his army uniform; Mr. Morton on the beach with a deep tan in the 1950s; Mr. Morton in a drama troupe in the Catskills; Mr. Morton in a suit and tie at the Rainbow Room.)* Ahhh. Here's to you, Mr. Morton. Here's to you. *(Downs his shot, takes a photo in hand.)* Mr. Morton, you were a very elegant man, weren't you?

Yesiree. *(He looks at the photo.)* A very elegant man. *(Mr. Morton now sits up, takes the sheet off of himself, removes his sunglasses.)*

MR. MORTON. Honey, I was gorgeous. *(Sheehy tries to cover his absolute panic.)*

SHEEHY. OK Sheehy — control. Control. I didn't hear anything.

MR. MORTON. I said I was gorgeous. *(Mr. Morton sits up, causally, and starts to chat with Sheehy. Who stays rigid, frozen in position.)* To look at me now, you'd have no idea but I was The Belle of the Ball. You could take me anywhere, and everyone did. *(Sheehy doesn't say anything.)* I was a walker before anyone knew what it was. *(Sheehy doesn't know what a walker is. Or maybe he's just in complete shock because A CORPSE IS TALKING TO HIM.)* You still don't know what that is, do you? A walker is … the perfect escort. Or weekend guest. A clean-shaven beard. *(Singing now.)* Tall and tan and young and lovely.

SHEEHY. I —

MR. MORTON. Don't just stand there, young Jack. Pour us a drink. And for pity sake, not that whiskey you've been swilling. It's summer: I never wore white before Memorial Day, and I never drank scotch until after Labor Day. Simple rules to live by, young Jack. Our gin is on the top shelf, tonic below. Top shelf gin, bottom shelf tonic. Get it? *(Sheehy nods.)* Then get them. We don't have all day. At least I don't. Allez allez. Drinks for everyone. Morton's final call. *(Sheehy finds the gin, just where Morton said it would be. And the tonic.)* You'll find two very gay summer tumblers next to the … what did you call it?, piñata bowl of meds here. *(Sheehy grabs the tumblers, pours two drinks. He's afraid to hand the drink to Morton.)* Go ahead, I won't bite. *(Takes the drink.)* Ice? Is, I'm afraid, a bit of a problem. The ice man cometh not. We'll have to rough it. Barbaric I know, but what can one do. It's so hard getting good help nowadays. And bring us a ciggie while you're at it. That is, if there's any left.

SHEEHY. I'm sorry. I —

MR. MORTON. Please. They are life's last little pleasure. Or afterlife's, in this case. Smoke'm if you got 'em, we used to say, in the war. And oh I loved them. *(Sheehy lights one for him as Morton says this. Morton takes a deep drag.)* Ahh. That's better … *(He exhales languorously.)* I'm supposed to quit, but I don't think it's an issue anymore. *(He offers Sheehy his cigarette. Sheehy declines.)*

SHEEHY. No thanks. I quit. Today was just a … Don't even miss 'em most of the —

MR. MORTON. Liar. I quit ten years ago. After the first bypass. And not a day went by in those ten years when I didn't think, "Oh, I want one." Little by little I had to give up everything. Boys: That was easy, actually. Life just got simpler … and quieter. Drink: not a drop until these last few weeks. Then, and this was insult to injury, they had me give up the sun. It was summer, and I was a ghost … that's when I knew. I was not long for this *(He sighs, way over the top.)* Veil of Tears …

SHEEHY. You shouldn't talk like that, Mr. Mor —

MR. MORTON. Ahh but the last few weeks of ciggies, and gin and tonics were divine. I only wish, since my valve was going to blow no matter what, that I had started to smoke and drink … sooner.

SHEEHY. You don't mean that.

MR. MORTON. But I do. And I am speaking from a position of knowledge. From the beyond. Or at least the en-route. If that bus ever gets here.

SHEEHY. *(Bonding.)* Tell me about it.

MR. MORTON. A bus — how mortifying. Couldn't we at least call it a jitney? *(They share a laugh. Morton takes Sheehy in, senses somehow Sheehy is the more dead of the two. Appalled, he now tries to talk to him, in an almost fatherly way.)* Have you ever been anywhere? Done any one?

SHEEHY. I've sewed my wild oats. If that's what you —

MR. MORTON. Your "wild oats"? That's priceless. How terribly, awfully quaint. And utterly beside the point. Have you lived your life?

SHEEHY. What do you mean?

MR. MORTON. Why do I get the feeling that if the bus ever comes, it's fifty-fifty they'll leave me and take you.

SHEEHY. That's e —

MR. MORTON. Or maybe they'll double us up. Two for the price of one. Special for the holiday weekend.

SHEEHY. This is great. Just great. Spend Fourth of July in a six story walk-up with a dead fairy. And he rags on me.

MR. MORTON. I'm not trying to "rag on you," young Jack. And there's no need to get mean. I am serious. Neither of us wanted to be here today, but I had very little choice in the matter. Woke up, made my bed, and I was dead. Tra la. But you, you're hardly even thirty.

SHEEHY. I'm twenty-six.

MR. MORTON. Really? It's worse than I thought. Time is not your friend young Jack. You shouldn't be cooped up with me in those polyester pants and those awful shoes. You should be *en vacance,* in the south of France. Or Majorca —

SHEEHY. Yuh. France. Real ef'n likely.

MR MORTON. Or Fire Island, or … Jones Beach. Soaking up the sun. Lying in the sand. A cooler full of —

SHEEHY. The sun's very bad for you —

MR. MORTON. WITH A COOLER FULL OF GIN, JACK. These are the best years of your life and you are pissing them away.

SHEEHY. Who the hell are you to —

MR. MORTON. I know life.

SHEEHY. Who the hell are you to tell me anything. Guys like you, who just did whatever you wanted, no family, no obligations, just frittered your life away, you turn around and —

MR. MORTON. There was that nasty little war, but-

SHEEHY. You turn around and judge me and the choices I've made —

MR. MORTON. Choices? You've lived twenty-six years and you haven't made one choice yet.

SHEEHY. OK that's it.

MR. MORTON. I know this isn't easy, son.

SHEEHY. Shut up.

MR. MORTON. But everything you do is so your dad won't think you're a nancy boy —

SHEEHY. I SAID SHUT UP!

MR. MORTON. So the guys won't —

SHEEHY. OK THAT'S IT — ENOUGH!

MR. MORTON. — so the boys in the blue wall won't think you're a pansy —

SHEEHY. *(Overlapping.)* I said THAT'S IT! SHUT UP! SHUT UP! SHUT UP! GO TO HELL YOU OLD QUEER! *(And with that, a chill suddenly passes through the room and Mr. Morton stops. Dead. His body returns to its lifeless repose.)* Mr. Morton? MR. MORTON. Mr. Morton! *(No response.)* What the hell is your problem? Giving me a — I don't have enough people telling me what to do, I have to hear it from a corpse. *(He looks at Morton.)* A corpse. I'm talking to a corpse. That's a good one. Huh. Dead man talking. I'm sitting here shouting at a dead man. If the guys at the station heard that, they'd lock me up. *(Realizes this is true, tries to understand what is happening. He shakes it off. It's just a dream. Relooks at the corpse. In Mr. Morton's clenched left hand, a gay tumbler, half full of gin and tonic.)* OK. Very funny. This is a good one guys. A real good one. And you're a good actor, Mr. Morton. I get it. This whole thing is like some sort of initiation. And I'm like, the world's biggest patsy. OK. Where's the camera? Come out guys. Nice job Mr — *(The downstairs buzzer rings. Loud. Sheehy jumps. It rings again. He goes to the intercom.)* Yeah? *(The buzzer rings again.)* Hello? *(Buzzer rings again.)* OK. The joke's over. C'mon up. I'm onto it. *(He buzzes them in. Then drops down to Mr. Morton. Tries to slap him out of it.)* C'mon. You've made your point. It's been very funny. But, before they get here — *(He tries to pry the gin glass out of Morton's hand. It's impossible.)* Mr. Morton. Mr. Morton. Please. They're coming. *(He can't pull the glass away.)* C'mon. C'mon. Please, Mr. Morton … give me that glass. *(He hears footsteps.)* Please. They're almost here. Please. Please. *(He breaks down and sobs. Mr. Morton's head gently rocks forward. His body now bends over as well, and he slowly doubles over on top of Sheehy, pinning him in a Pieta-like embrace.)* Please. *(There's a loud, almost supernatural knock on the door. Blackout.)*

End of Play

PROPERTY LIST

Police walkie-talkie
Notepad
Phone
Answering machine
Stacks of books
Hand towel
Stack of Playbills
Helmut Newton Photo Book
Latex glove
Pack of Pall Mall cigarettes
Deck of cards
Sunglasses
Lighter or matches
Big clay bowl of prescription pills in their containers
Glasses, decanters of Scotch, gin, etc.
Photos
Bedsheet
"Gay" bright gin and tonic tumblers
Intercom
"Sealed by Order of Police Department" sticker
Watch (Cartier)
Holster with gun
Piles of clothes
tchotchke
Tonic

SOUND EFFECTS

Toilet flushing
Phone ringing
Answering machine beep
Outgoing message on machine
Caller's voice on machine
Noise of flatulence
Retching
Firecrackers
Buzzer
Footsteps
Loud "almost supernatural" knock on door

UNITED

CHARACTERS

ERIN — The 30-something married sister of Bobby. Pretty but past caring.

BOBBY — A handsome homosexual. Dashing and self-assured.

ALEEM — Bobby's boyfriend. British, well-educated.

BROOKE SHIELDS (if available)

UNITED

*Airport. Lounge. Erin holds a hand made sign that reads
"Brooke Shields" on one side. She scans the crowd. Doesn't see
Bobby coming down the stairs. He sees her.*

BOBBY. E.J.!
ERIN. Bobby. *(She turns, they hug. He sees the sign.)*
BOBBY. "Brooke Shields"? *(She flips the sign over, on the other side
it says "Bobby.")*
ERIN. The cops let the limo driver double park when they saw it.
You look great.
BOBBY. Don't I? I mean, you too. Brunette is this year's brown. I
got you this. *(He hands her a Paris Hilton T-shirt.)*
ERIN. Paris Hilton?
BOBBY. Her show is brilliant. Brechtian in its indictment of our
class system — *(She hands him the shirt back.)*
ERIN. Save it for your blog. What's the big news.
BOBBY. What makes you think there's big news.
ERIN. You told me to set up a dinner with Mom and Dad. You
wouldn't tell me why. You flew in on one day's notice —
BOBBY. For the holidays.
ERIN. What holiday.
BOBBY. ... Sukkoth
ERIN. We're not Jewish, Bobby.
BOBBY. I know. It would have been so much easier. I hate being
Unitarian. It's so non-dogmatically dogmatic. You know. You're
welcome to believe anything you want to believe, as long as you
respect the beliefs of everyone else. And try to do good. What kind
of a clap trap religion is that. It's so free it's repressive.
ERIN. You didn't check bags did you?
BOBBY. They made me. I said it would fit in the overhead, but
they said for security reasons we're only allowed one carry-on. And
I asked what difference it made for security if the bag with the
bomb in it was in the overhead, or checked.

ERIN. You didn't.
BOBBY. I should have. I didn't. It's the story of my life. How's Wilbur.
ERIN. His name is Wilton. He's fine. Thank you. The second he heard you were coming he —
BOBBY. Made plans to work late?
ERIN. NO. He got the air mattress out of storage.
BOBBY. Isn't that thoughtless? No need. We're staying at a hotel.
ERIN. We? Is that royal?
BOBBY. He is, I'm not.
ERIN. Who.
BOBBY. My betrothed. He's some sort of Prince. Or —
ERIN. You're getting married?
BOBBY. Don't say it that way.
ERIN. You're getting married!
BOBBY. We are. P-town. Next weekend. And it finally pays to be Unitarian. I have my choice of like, eighteen different ministers. Lesbian. Transgendered. But I want you to give me away. Please say yes.
ERIN. Yes. But, to whom?
BOBBY. To my Prince — He should be here any minute. Flying in from London.
ERIN. You're not back with Arnold.
BOBBY. His name was Arthur, and god no. The second gay marriage became legalized, or semi-legalized, or quasi-decriminalized, or whatever it is, he freaked out. "I can't commit. I'm not ready. You deserve better." He kept saying it over and over, so finally I just told him he was right.
ERIN. You didn't. Good for you.
BOBBY. I didn't. I should have. He left. Took four hundred dollars, my Cartier watch that Grandpa left, and all my anti-depressants.
ERIN. Where do you meet these boys.
BOBBY. At meat markets. Where do you think.
ERIN. And your Prince?
BOBBY. At a crop circle.
ERIN. Is that one of those gay things that maybe I don't want to know about —
BOBBY. South western England. These enormous crop circles. Incredible patterns six, seven football fields in size, just ... crop up, over night —
ERIN. I thought Cable TV proved those were fakes.

30

BOBBY. Not these. Some of them are. The fake ones. They're obvious. Crudely hewn, no sense of design, or flow. Like something you'd buy at Today's Man. But the real ones, they're other worldly, Erin. The detail. It's cross-hatched. Like braided bread. That's what I said when I saw them. I blurted it out. And he looked at me and said "Taslajarah?" *(He waits for her to understand the significance of this. And waits.)* Taslajarah?
ERIN. I get it, the bread. Right.
BOBBY. You are getting so reductive. The bread, it's braided. The strands, separate, coming together as one.
ERIN. Paris Hilton and Kahil Gilbran? Bobby, you've got to get out of L.A.
BOBBY. We stayed up all night, hoping to see a crop circle form. But —
ERIN. A watched crop never boils?
BOBBY. We've been together ever since. Except for when he travels. You'll like him. I know you will, he's ... spiritual. And not just because he's — *(Aleem comes down the stairs now. He's in a bad mood.)*
ALEEM. Bobby!
BOBBY. Aleem. *(Bobby hugs Aleem. Erin seems very uncomfortable in Aleem's presence, although he's so angry, he doesn't notice her. As he rants, [in a slight British accent, his back to Erin], Bobby tries to calm him.)*
ALEEM. These little bureaucratic bastards. Two hours. Two hours at Customs. I have a green card, I have my own business, I've lived here for fifteen fecking years, I fly back and forth every two months, and my name they tell me is the same name as some one on their watch list so I show them the State Department letter that tells them I am not to be confused with Mr. Aleem Al Terrorzizi and still they keep me four hours — no food, no phone — in a crowded pea green room that smells like bad cheese until someone somewhere confirms to them that India is neither Arab nor part of the Axis of Evil and they finally give me my belt and shoelaces back and when they let me go I yelled, "You want to know why your jobs are being outsourced to my country, it's because you people are fecking idiots who can't even read your own mother tongue."
BOBBY. You didn't.
ALEEM. I didn't. But I should have. My god they're absolute morons. Do we have time to get a good Roger in at the hotel before our stupid dinner with your —
BOBBY. Aleem, this is my sister — *(Aleem stops, turns now. Puts his hand out.)*

31

ALEEM. Oh. Pleased to — *(He finally takes her in, seems completely thrown, then recovers.)* — meet you …

BOBBY. — Erin. E.J. this is —

ERIN. Aleem. *(She shakes his hand. There is an awkward silence.)*

ALEEM. Well. Shall we go.

BOBBY. They made me check my carry-on. Let me see if it's coming up yet. You two just … continue hitting it off. *(He goes to the baggage claim, leaving Aleem and Erin alone.)*

ALEEM. It was really barbaric, Erin. These women were, I swear to God, ululating and —

ERIN. How've you been.

ALEEM. The last ten years? Up and down. Does he know …

ERIN. Did you tell him?

ALEEM. I didn't know.

ERIN. You didn't know you were "rogering" my brother.

ALEEM. Oh, I knew that. I didn't know he was your brother.

ERIN. You didn't remember I had a brother named Bobby.

ALEEM. There's a lot of Bobby's in the world, Erin. And he always refers to you as E.J. And you never even told me your brother was gay.

ERIN. Well then. We're even. You never told me you were gay.

ALEEM. I wasn't. I mean, after we broke up, that's when I started to date men.

ERIN. Thanks. That makes me feel so much better.

ALEEM. I didn't mean it was your fault. I — I had so much self-loathing — to be gay, in my culture, it — Oh look, there's Brooke Shields. *(Brooke Shields walks across the concourse. Erin doesn't turn to see her.)*

ERIN. Don't change the subject, Aleem.

ALEEM. I wasn't trying to —

ERIN. I hated when you used to do that.

ALEEM. *(Changing the subject, re: her ring.)* So, you're married?

ERIN. Don't change the — *(Gives up.)* Yes.

ALEEM. Good.

ERIN. We didn't break up. You left.

ALEEM. It's ten years ago Erin. Let's not —

ERIN. Nine actually. I remember because it was your birthday. I threw my roommates out for the night. I cleaned the house. God I scrubbed every inch of it. I took two months of my waitress tips and cooked, I still remember the menu —

ALEEM. I don't think we —

ERIN. Avocado and salmon, a north-south salad like the one we

32

had in Paris. Veal chops, even though I was a vegetarian. Hand cut french fries. Sauteed broccoli rabe.

ALEEM. I should have called.

ERIN. And a 1979 Brunello. The man at the wine store told me to let it breathe for a few hours. And I did, I opened it at six, and let it breathe until midnight. And then I drank it. One glass at a time, saving some, in case you ever showed up. I called the emergency rooms, I called your friends. I humiliated myself at two different college campuses in one night. Williams and Amherst. You just … disappeared.

ALEEM. I thought I sent a post card. Didn't I? I'm sure I—

ERIN. Of what, a crop circle? I don't think so. I don't think I ever heard from you again. And I wondered, for years, what was wrong with me. Who did you leave me for? What did she have that I didn't have? How could I trust someone, love someone, who could care so little about me. Was I that unworthy of love?

ALEEM. You know, obviously, I liked you. A lot. Just the wrong … I mean, I ended up with your brother. So, clearly, it wasn't you. I adored you. I just didn't want to live a lie.

ERIN. That's funny.

ALEEM. What.

ERIN. I kind of wish you had told me. Before I met Wilton.

ALEEM. Your husband. I'm looking forward to —

ERIN. Snuff it. After I finished the Brunello, it was very good, by the way — I ended up going to a bar. And I needed a cigarette, thank you very much, and I bummed it from a little loser of a guy. Wilton. Wilton isn't charming like you. Or smart like you. Or exotic like you. What Wilton was, is, will always be, is … stable. A little heavy, a little sweaty, a little bald. And he drove me home that night. And he kept checking in on me. Through my depression. My little sleeping pill incident. After I dropped out. Through a few more train wrecks. He just kept calling. And finally I told myself, stable is good. Stable won't drop out of college in his senior year and disappear off the face of the earth. Stable won't leave you, for another woman. Stable will never ever get near enough to your heart to break it. And now, after nine years, I find out, the reason you left me, had nothing to do with me. You left me, because you didn't want to live a lie, but you didn't have the balls to tell me that, so I ended up, living a lie. And you end up marrying my brother. And I'm supposed to give him away to you. This isn't my life, it's a goddamned O'Henry story.

ALEEM. Erin. I'm sorry. I was ... I was scared. Please, your brother and I —

ERIN. Aleem. I've waited nine years to say this: Fuck you. *(Bobby, bag in hand, now returns from baggage claim.)*

BOBBY. Hey guys, you're not going to believe this. I just saw Brooke Shields, at the — *(Sees they are not in a playful mood.)* Is everything OK?

ALEEM. It's been a long day, Bobby. *(They start to walk out. Erin stays behind.)*

BOBBY. E.J., are you alright.

ERIN. Yeah. I was trying to figure out if Aleem and I knew each other. From college days. We should have, but, we didn't. It turns out, there was no connection. *(To Aleem.)* No connection at all. *(Bobby puts his arm around Aleem, they walk out, as Erin picks up Bobby's carry-on. Waits. Then follows them out.)*

End of Play

PROPERTY LIST

Hand-made sign saying Brooke Shields on one side; Bobby on other side
Paris Hilton T-shirt
Carry-on bag

HAPPY FOR YOU

CHARACTERS

BILL — Very expressive, somewhat flamboyant.

TONY — African-American. Urban cool.

CARRIE — Sexy actress.

PEG — Bitter, sardonic theater type.

RON — Jaded writer.

HAPPY FOR YOU

Bill's rent stabilized living room, on Oscar night. Bill is on the phone. Ron is getting very drunk. Tony watches the TV. Bill is also the keeper of the Oscar pool cheat sheets.

BILL. I got his machine.

TONY. Of course you got his machine, he's at the Oscars.

BILL. *(Into machine.)* Hi Roy, we're all here, watching, and your category is coming up, and we're so excited, and in your honor we exempted your category from the betting pool because we know you're definitely going to win, and we just want you to know, that when you do win, we're your real friends and we all knew it all along. And we're so happy for you so don't forget us now that you're famous and also, Tony says kiss Kevin Spacey for him, on the lips.

TONY. *(Yelling.)* Kyra Sedgwick, not Kevin Spacey.

BILL. *(Still on phone, but now sees.)* Oh my god. There he is! Roy, you're on TV right now. We're all waving. *(Bill waves. Peg and Carrie come in from the kitchen with food, beers. Rush to the TV screen.)*

CARRIE. Where! Where. I don't see him.

PEG. There. Five rows above Matt Damon. Next to the cleavage.

TONY. *(Staring.)* That's not Matt Damon, it's the other one. Who had amnesia. *(Peg and Carrie look at him.)*

CARRIE. Hon, Matt Damon's the one who had amnesia.

BILL. People, I don't have my x-ray glasses. *(He gestures at Tony, Carrie, and Peg, until they settle. Carrie joins Tony. Peg goes to Ron.)*

RON. Beer?

PEG. Another? *(He puts his hand out. Gets what looks like his sixth of the evening, from Peg, who then sits with him.)*

CARRIE. I cannot believe that girl he's with.

TONY. Where have I seen her face before?

PEG. On a milk carton. She's a child.

CARRIE. Stop.

BILL. Honestly, he's lucky there isn't an Amber Alert out for her.

CARRIE. *(Staring at the screen.) What* is she wearing?

PEG. A haz-mat suit?

BILL. Orange is so ... orange.

CARRIE. She looks like an underage hooker.

PEG. I can't believe he's not embarrassed to be seen with her.

TONY. There is no word for embarrassment in the L.A. dictionary.

RON. I think she's kind of cute. *(Carrie, Peg, and Bill look at him.)*

BILL. *(To Peg.)* All right, I give up. Your boyfriend really is straight.

CARRIE. God, poor Marcie, can you imagine? She's all alone.

PEG. We should call her.

RON. And say what? That we just saw her ex at the Oscar's fondling the seventeen-year-old cheese ball he met on the set while she was home looking after his parents.

TONY. Ouch.

CARRIE. Look. She's better off without him.

BILL. Absolutely, I mean, who would want to be engaged to an Academy-award-winning writer with a house in Brentwood when they could be sharing a one bedroom with two lesbians in Washington Heights.

RON. Nominated.

BILL. What?

RON. He hasn't won yet.

PEG. He's going to win, Ron.

RON. Right.

CARRIE. It's kind of a lock: a sweet little movie that won't win any other awards, plus the *Times* did that big article on him two weeks ago.

RON. You mean four big articles. Which I'm sure has nothing to do with his Uncle.

PEG. Not that you're bitter.

RON. Why would I be bitter? *(Everyone looks at him.)*

BILL. Here's the documentary short. Everyone. Shh shh shh. *(They all watch the little clips. Everyone is moved by the clips in unison, except Ron. After Clip one:)*

ALL but RON. Ohhhh. *(After Clip two:)* Awww. *(After Clip three:)* Ha ha ha.

BILL. And the winner is ... No wait, the Oscar goes to ... *(They wait. Lean in. Lean back. It's no surprise.) Simone, the Tender Story of One Girl's Flight to Freedom Under the Nazis.* Well, there's a shock. Who else had it? *(Bill, Carrie, Peg, and Ron raise their hands.)*

RON. *(To Tony.)* Tell me you voted for the March on Selma movie.

TONY. Shut up.

RON. Bet with your head, not your heart.

BILL. It's still a tie. Three ways.

TONY. Maybe we *should* count our votes in Roy's category.

CARRIE. Why? We all voted for him. Didn't we? *(The others look at Ron, who sips his beer.)*

TONY. Do you think he'll thank us, in the speech?

BILL. Absolutely. He loves us.

CARRIE. He told me he hasn't even written a speech. Doesn't want to jinx it. *(Tony reacts to this.)*

TONY. I didn't know you were speaking to him.

CARRIE. He calls me once in a while. Or e-mails. It's no big —

TONY. Does Marcie know you're speaking to him?

BILL. Anyone for salsa?

CARRIE. I didn't want to upset her. I'm sure he only calls me because I'm close to her and he likes the connection. *(Everyone looks at her.)* What?

PEG. I can't believe he hasn't written a speech. He looks so calm.

RON. Oh please. He's been working on his acceptance speech since we went to NYU. The first time we were assigned a two person dialogue, he wrote an imaginary interview between himself and that asshole with the beard from the Actor's Studio.

BILL. *(To Peg.)* Is he always this upbeat?

RON. I'm just saying, he has a speech. And I bet he leaves us out and kisses every ass in Hollywood, including Harvey's.

PEG. Here we go.

CARRIE. He hates Harvey. It's all he talks about.

TONY. How often do you e-mail him?

CARRIE. Harvey tried to make him change the ending of his film. And he told Harvey he'd take his name off before he'd make the change.

RON and TONY. And you believe that?

PEG. Let's not —

RON. His movie ends with the ghetto chess team winning the championship, and their dedicated coach finding out that the girl he had thought was lost forever had loved him all along, even though she's a supermodel and he's a substitute teacher who lives with his disabled Mom. What part of that sappy, unbelievably fake ending would Harvey possibly want him to change?

CARRIE. I thought you didn't see the movie.

RON. I didn't. I just read about it in the *Times.* Over and

PEG. *(Overlapping with Ron.)* LET.

RON. Over and —

PEG. IT.

RON. *(Overlapping.)* Over and —

PEG. GO! I mean, Jesus. Enough! *(She can't stop herself.)* At least he finished his screenplay. *(Room now goes quiet. For a very long uncomfortable time.)*

BILL. *(Singing more or less to himself upstage.)* Who's afraid of Virginia Woolf, Virginia Woolf, Virginia —

CARRIE. *(To Ron.)* Roy said your notes on his script really … helped him, Ron.

RON. *(Getting up.)* Did he? *(Walks out.)* More beers anyone? *(Ron walks out. Conversation now turns increasingly disconnected.)*

TONY. *(To Carrie.)* Do you guys e-mail once a day. Twice?

CARRIE. *(To Peg.)* He really did say the notes were great.

BILL. And yet, somehow I don't think that makes Ron feel better.

CARRIE. Oh, give it a rest. I mean, do you always have to be such a big fag? *(Bill is hurt by this.)*

PEG. It was bad enough when he found out the movie was getting made. But after it won Sundance …

CARRIE. He really never saw it?

RON. *(Entering.)* Nope. *(Hands a beer to Tony, keeps one for himself. Sits back down. No one says anything.)* Do you guys want me to go back out, so you can finish talking about me. *(No one answers.)* Has he won yet?

BILL. It's just coming up now. Oh my god, Ethan Hawke is giving out the award.

PEG. Ethan Hawke?

CARRIE. He *is* a novelist —

TONY. Are you … emailing him, too? *(Tony looks at Carrie. Carrie and Bill lean in. Peg looks at Ron, who stares straight ahead.)*

BILL. He must be dying.

RON. *(To himself.)* We're all —

BILL. Ab-so-lute-ly dying.

RON. *(To himself.)* — So happy for you.

CARRIE. Look at her, holding his hand. That is so tacky.

BILL. This is it. And … the Oscar goes to … *(They all lean in. Each in their own world. Hold for a frozen beat. Blackout.)*

End of Play

42

PROPERTY LIST

Snacks, beers
Phone
TV

NINE-TEN

CHARACTERS

LYRIS TOUZET — a new-age spiritualist dancer. Great body.

JOHN McCORMACK — Handsome leading man. Straight arrow

KEARRIE WHITMAN — Killer stock broker. Still wears power suits

LESLIE RUDIN — 30-something New Yorker. Hyper.

NICK THERON — African American. A realist.

COURT OFFICER — 40s, a lifer.

NINE-TEN

Jury Duty Grand Hall. Morning. John, a slightly awkward bond trader, sits on a bench. Very neat, buttoned down. He reads a perfectly folded Wall Street Journal. Lyris Touzet, a dancer, enters, almost spills her coffee on him.

LYRIS. Is this Part B?
JOHN. What.
LYRIS. Part B, or not part B?
JOHN. Ah ... that is the question.
LYRIS. Are you making fun of me?
JOHN. No no. Um, let me look at your ... *(She hands him a slip of paper, he reads it.)* Where you are is where you're supposed to be. *(She sits next to him. He needs a little more personal space than she does.)*
LYRIS. Why do they call us at eight-thirty? It's like, nine already, and they haven't said anything.
JOHN. They build in a grace period.
LYRIS. They what?
JOHN. They say eight-thirty so that most people get here by nine. And around nine ten they start calling names.
LYRIS. You knew this, and you came at eight-thirty?
JOHN. Eight actually.
LYRIS. Eight A.M.? You must hate your wife.
JOHN. I don't see her much. We both have to be at work at six.
LYRIS. You punch in at six?
JOHN. Well, I don't ... punch in exactly. But, the desk opens at six so ...
LYRIS. Your desk opens?
JOHN. Sorry. Trading desk. Bonds. Euros, mostly. From my desk, I'm up so high, on a clear day, you can see Europe. *(At a bench opposite, Nick Theron works the* Times *crossword puzzle as Leslie Rudin arrives, pissed off and hyper.)*
LESLIE. Part B?
NICK. Must be.

LESLIE. Have they called any —

NICK. Does it look like it? *(She looks to the court officer's desk, downstage left.)* Every once in a while this guy comes out and says we should wait. Which is … helpful.

LESLIE. I tried to get out of it on the phone and they said it was my third postponement and I had to come down here in person on the day of and that I wasn't going to get out anyway. And I finally get here — do they just change the names of the subway lines for spite lately? — and there's a line a mile long to get through security and they go through my purse like I'm a serial killer and it turns out if I want to smoke I'm going to have to go down and outside, and then wait on line again for them to check my bag. This just sucks.

NICK. I'm going to tell the judge, that I'm a felon. He won't even question it. And he'll tell me felons can't serve. I'll act offended at this. And then he'll just let me go back to my life.

LESLIE. *(Impressed.)* That's good.

NICK. Racial profiling. A two way street. *(Over to John and Lyris.)*

LYRIS. My brother's in the same building. Security guard. You probably don't know him. *(Kearrie, a tough business woman enters, rushed.)*

KEARRIE. Part B?

LYRIS and JOHN. Or not part b?

KEARRIE. It's too early for cute. *(They look at her, she means it.)* Have they started to give out postponements yet?

LYRIS. No one gets a postponement.

KEARRIE. I'm on a flight tomorrow. *(Pulls something out of her bag.)* I've got a ticket. *(John takes another look at her.)*

JOHN. Kearrie?

KEARRIE. What?

JOHN. It's me, John …

KEARRIE. Right. John. That narrows it down.

JOHN. John McCormack. From Wharton. *(Kearrie still doesn't place him.)*

LYRIS. *(To John.)* You sure leave an impression.

JOHN. Story of my life. *(To Kearrie.)* Case study: euro-economic unity.

KEARRIE. You got an A, I got a B plus. Even though we worked together.

JOHN. *(To Lyris.)* You know about Irish Alzheimer's … you forget everything except your grudges.

KEARRIE. You went to Gold and Strauss when we graduated,

right?

JOHN. Still there.

KEARRIE. *(Grades him a loser.)* You're kidding. You are not still at —

JOHN. Just the last ten years. Kearrie this is —

LYRIS. Lyris Touzet. Spiritual dancer. And healer.

JOHN. Lyris this is Kearrie Whitman. We went to Wharton together. Class of '91.

LYRIS. I must have missed you two by like ... one year. *(Leslie and Nick. He has no hope of attending to his crossword puzzle. Leslie must talk or die.)*

LESLIE. I'm out in the Hamptons. One week after Labor Day. Paradise found. The assholes are gone. The beaches are empty. The water is warm.

NICK. Sharks are hungry.

LESLIE. No sharks in the Hamptons. Professional courtesy.

NICK. Touché.

LESLIE. I think, I'll stay another day. Then I remember ... fuck me — eight-thirty summons. Drive in at midnight. Get stuck in traffic. The L.I.E. has got to be the only road in the world that has traffic jams at two a.m. By the time I get to my garage it's locked for the night. You ever try to find a space on the right side of the street at two A.M.? *(Back to: John and Lyris chatting. Kearrie plays with her Palm Pilot.)*

JOHN. It's funny, I always wanted to be a spiritual dancer.

LYRIS. You're making fun of me.

JOHN. I'm not ... swear to god. But what is a —

LYRIS. I heal people, through movement. Rhythm. Every person has their own ... pulse. Below the surface, that —

KEARRIE. Fuck me!

LYRIS. I help them to get in touch with their inner —

KEARRIE. *(Turns to them.)* Fuck me fuck me fuck ...

JOHN. What's hers? *(Kearrie now rants in their direction, about her Palm Pilot.)*

KEARRIE. Money on the table. I've got a watch list. It's programmed to signal me when there's a discrepancy between euro prices and ADRs. The spread is sitting there. Sitting there. It's blinking — buy me. Buy me. I try to buy and my damn signal fades. What's the point of fucking having a watch list if you can't follow up on it. This whole building should be wired. This city is ... in the stone ages.

LYRIS. *(To John.)* Some people are harder cases than others. *(Over to Nick and Leslie.)*

NICK. My neighborhood, downtown, they're *always* filming. Some sequel to a sequel to a disaster flick. *Mortal Danger Times Four.* Whatever. Which means like —

LESLIE. They take every parking place. Big lights up —

NICK. — all night long.

LESLIE. Idiots in walkie-talkies saying don't walk there. On your own street. Call the cops to complain, they don't care. No one in this city cares. The film crew can be, like, setting off concussion bombs, and nobody does anything. *(Back to:)*

JOHN. *(To Lyris.)* I can't.

LYRIS. Everybody can move. Even you ... Stand up. *(He doesn't. Loud:)* STAND UP! *(Nick and Leslie hear this. Look over to John and Lyris. John doesn't want to attract attention, so he stands. John and Lyris now overlap with Nick and Leslie, Kearrie is in her own world. To John:)* Just start to, sway a little ... from your hips.

LESLIE. *(To Nick.)* That is sick the way he's flirting with her. *(John sits back down.)*

JOHN. I can't.

LYRIS. Yes you can.

NICK. *(To Leslie.)* How do you know it's his fault?

LESLIE. *(To Nick.)* It's always the guy's fault. I date cops. Believe me. I know.

JOHN. *(To Lyris.)* I don't like to. Move. I like things as they are. I've had the same job for ten years.

KEARRIE. *(On her cell phone, to her office.)* Here? It's a fucking hell hole. What do you think? Ah-huh. Ah-huh. Ah-huh. Look — keep that on hold.

JOHN. *(To Lyris, oblivious to Kearrie.)* Same office, same view. Married my junior high school sweetheart. We take the same train to work. We have the same lunch. Tuna. On rye. No mayo.

LYRIS. No mayo?

JOHN. It's not so bad, once you get used to it.

KEARRIE. *(Into phone.)* Yeah as soon as they call roll, I show my plane ticket ... and I'm out of here. *(Now, from downstage left, a Court Officer enters.)*

COURT OFFICER. Hello folks. Welcome to New York County Jury Duty. Before you all come up to me —

KEARRIE. Excuse me, I have a flight to —

NICK. I have a record —

COURT OFFICER. *(He drowns her out.)* — with your reasons for why you shouldn't be here, let me tell you: I've heard them all. On the bright side, most of you will get to go back to your life in two or three days. *(Leslie, Nick, Kearrie, John, and Lyris all groan. Two days is eternity.)* And we are as happy to have you, as you are happy to be here. First things first. Check your summons, and be sure you're in the right place. This is Civil Court. Part B. Sixty Centre Street. Today is Monday, September tenth ... two thousand and one. *(Blackout.)*

End of Play

PROPERTY LIST

Wall Street Journal
Take-out coffee
Slip of paper
Times crossword puzzle
Airline ticket
Palm Pilot
Cellphone

FEAR NETWORK NEWS

CHARACTERS

DENA — Gorgeous, fit, aggressive blonde co-anchor of *Fear Network News.*

SCOTT — Handsome, fit, aggressive male co-anchor of *Fear Network News.*

JUSTIN — Young hunky reporter with an agenda. Doubles as GUARD.

TRISHNAYA — Young African-American retail assistant at The Gap. Doubles as GUARD.

FARHED "TOM" HOMRIZI — Preppy Arab-American.

ANNIE FACTUAL — Frizzy-haired, button wearing, student/activist.

FEAR NETWORK NEWS

The casual set of Fear Network News. Anchors (or hosts, actually) Scott and Dena sit and swivel in Aeron chairs, no desk. She's blonde, thin, and wears a short skirt, crossing her long lean legs all the time. He has a lantern jaw, and is Chelsea Gym fit. They look at a monitor for updates, and interviews — which we see taking place live in various corners of the stage. There are two chairs for guests they interview. A low, broken bench for liberals, and one equal to theirs, for patriots. Big monumental important hip music as lights up on them. Sound note: As the music gives way, a newsroom background sound should be heard. Not the WINS news ticker sound — but rather individual words, overlapping, not completely audible until the end. The words: fear. Terror. Death. Germs. Anthrax. Weapons. Explosion. Bombs. Death. Fear. Terror. Terror. Bomb. It should sound digitized, or other worldly.

DENA. This is a *Fear Network News* Alert. — I'm Dena Troy.

SCOTT. I'm Scott Warman — you're watching *Fear Network News:* You give us six minutes, we'll scare the bejesus out of you — We've got breaking news tonight on the terror front. Let's jump right to it. Dena.

DENA. Scott, frightening reports are just coming in. And although information is fragmentary, it looks like we may be experiencing a major event tonight, one we've feared for a long time. Scott.

SCOTT. Now, Dena, we all know our government has done everything they can to protect us from these cave dwelling hoodlums —

DENA. And they've done an unbelievable job —

SCOTT. But the terrorists only had to get lucky once, and tonight, on the eve of our nation's election, they may, and I want to emphasize may, be on the verge of pulling off the unthinkable. Here's what we know so far. *(Dena and Scott look at monitor. One beat, two beats, wince and look away.)*

DENA. *(Looks to screen.)* The footage is grainy. Its provenance not yet determined, but if it's real, it's ... horrifying. Barbaric. Unthinkable.

SCOTT. And yet, not surprising, given the lack of humanity we've seen over and over again from these militant terrorist militants.

DENA. And their Sierra Club supporters.

SCOTT. Let's go to our *Fear Network News* reporters in the field now, for their fear imbalanced reports. Justin, can you hear me. *(Justin, who looks about 19, but hip and hunky, on location with a fast food worker outside a mall parking lot.)*

JUSTIN. Barely Scott. It's a mob scene here. As state militia, and local residents, brandishing their newly re-legalized semi-automatics, have arrived en masse at the roped off scene. With us is Trishnaya who works at a Gap in the Mall. Trishnaya, can you tell us your story.

TRISHNAYA. I was at the mall, and I left for my Taco Bell break, and I came back, and everything was cordoned off.

JUSTIN. Scary stuff. What happened next.

TRISHNAYA. I've just been hanging around. They won't let me back in.

JUSTIN. Have they given you any sort of time table.

TRISHNAYA. They said it could be anywhere from an hour to a week, to never. I'll have to wait it out.

DENA. Justin, it's Dena.

JUSTIN. Hi sweet pea. *(She smiles, all cute. Scott seems jealous. Dena gets back to work.)*

DENA. What can you or Trishnaya tell us about what if anything is going on. How terrifying is it.

JUSTIN. Very, Dena. Something, and I'm not sure what, is up. Security teams from everywhere have descended en masse. The air is heavy with the smell of sweat, and fear. The word among those who ask not to be quoted, is this could be the big one. And if it is the big one, it's not, according to those in a position to know and remain nameless, a coincidence that it may be taking place tonight.

DENA. You mean, because of tomorrow's election.

JUSTIN. Precisely. They hate us because of our democratic ideals. They hate us because our god is better than theirs. They just flat out don't like us. And they'd like nothing more than to see our freedoms destroyed. We're a long way from knowing what's happened here tonight, but let's not deceive ourselves. We've learned these monsters will do anything to manipulate us with fear and terror.

DENA. Indeed we have, Justin. Keep up the good work, and stay safe out there.

SCOTT. With us now, in our *Fear Network News* — you give us six minutes, we'll scare the bejesus out of you — studios, Professor Farhed "Tom" Homrizi, he's an Arab, but one of the good ones. And he's written several books on terror, and the threat from without, aided by those within our midst. Professor, good to have you with us — *(Dena waves as Farhed [a good looking, preppily dressed Arab-American] is escorted gently to his seat.)*
FARHED. Great to be back, Scott. Dena, you look lovely.
DENA. As good as seventy virgins in paradise?
FARHED. Absolutely. *(Scott, a little jealous, starts the interview.)*
SCOTT. Doesn't she? Now Farhed, if, as some people are now saying that what we fear has happened, has taken place, if they are right, how could it happen?
FARHED. There are no easy answers, Scott. Ours is a free and open society, and as such, it's a lightening rod for exactly this sort of mindless jihad.
DENA. Speaking of how free and open our society is, we have with us tonight someone who by all rights should be ashamed to show her face on a night when a tragedy of these dimensions may or may not be exploding. But in the interests of our fear-imbalanced coverage, welcome Annie Factual. She's a grad student in sociology from Queens College, the author of a series of articles in her school paper entitled, "It's Coming, It's Coming! Why Isn't Anyone Listening to Me? Does Everyone Think I'm Just Doing This for My Health?" *(Annie [frizzy haired, political button-wearing, slightly heavy college student] is brought out and physically seated on the uncomfortable liberal bench. [Note: Trishnaya and Justin can double as the "guards" for Farhed and Annie respectively. If they do, Trishnaya should be very gentle with Farhed, and Justin should be as abusive as possible.])* Annie, what do you have to say for yourself, given the tragedy that may be unfolding tonight, and given your writing, which some people say gives aid and comfort to the cowards who are responsible for what may have occurred.
ANNIE. I don't know if that's really fair —
DENA. And the slaughter of innocent Americans is, I suppose.
ANNIE. Well, no. But in my new term paper, "I Hate to Say I Told You So," I outline how, given our isolationist arrogance as a superpower, and our history of training those who later become our enemies, we should have seen this coming.
DENA. Blaming the victim. Sad when overweight women do that, isn't it Scott.

SCOTT. Terrible. Farhed, do you think we should have seen this coming.

FARHED. There's simply no way to predict the irrational.

SCOTT. That's what makes it irrational.

DENA. Farhed, as a follow-up. Could what may or may not have happened tonight, happen again?

FARHED. Absolutely.

ANNIE. Then you're predicting it, aren't you? *(She's glanced at, then ignored. When no one is looking, she's tasered by either Scott, or her guard.)*

DENA. Let me ask you both, how could this have happened? Farhed?

FARHED. I think, clearly, the Clinton administration is to blame for this. They ignored repeated warning signs, plus created an atmosphere of moral laxity, that could only lead to the sort of catastrophic tragedy that may be unfolding now. The problem was ignored, if not fostered under Clinton, and inherited by the current administration who could in no way have seen it coming.

ANNIE. I'm wondering, if the Clinton administration long out of power, stands accused, why couldn't the current administration also be accused of ignoring those warnings, or leading us into the wrong war, or —

DENA. That is such an unfair charge.

SCOTT. You're on an American cable network, young lady. Keep that in mind. Even our Arab friend here knows at a time like this, dissent is tantamount to treason, right professor?

FARHED. Absolutely. To engage in this sort of Monday morning quarterbacking, when our nation needs to come together, to rally around our strong and decisive leader, makes you as much a part of the problem, if not a cause of the problem, as the causers of this catastrophe.

ANNIE. Actually, given what we know now, it could just be the work of right wing terrorists.

DENA. Oh really. *(Dena [or guard] tasers Annie.)*

ANNIE. Or maybe even an accident … an act of God. *(Scott [or guard] tasers her again.)* Hey. *(Scott acts completely innocent.)*

FARHED. Actually, Mother Nature is a possibility.

SCOTT. Interesting. If it is her handiwork, could she do it again?

FARHED. Who?

SCOTT. Mother nature.

FARHED. Once she's crossed this threshold, gotten a taste of it, so to speak, then, the next time ... yes. I'm afraid so.

DENA. If it is Mother Nature, then we should hunt the bitch down and kill her. Which I believe is only a matter of time anyway.

SCOTT. Either way, Professor, what is the next step here. To keep our country safe.

FARHED. A two-tiered approach. First, over the next few days, we should sift through our database. See if in fact we knew this was coming, but did not act on it for fear of tipping someone or some group off to our intelligence.

ANNIE. What's the point of intelligence if we don't use it? *(Everyone looks at her. Scott [or guard] sneaks another taser shock in. Whenever she gets out of line, she risks a shock. After a while, she anticipates them, and then they don't come. Until she lets her guard down, and they renew.)*

DENA. And your second tier, professor.

FARHED. I understand it's already being put in place — a temporary suspension of the electoral process until these madmen are hunted down and captured.

ANNIE. It's being put in place? Isn't that —

SCOTT. We ask the questions here, young lady.

DENA. When these godless anti-democratic heathens, and I'm not talking about all Arabs here, Professor —

FARHED. Thank you.

DENA. When they, and their liberal sympathizers are finally pulled from their caves — as I understand some trade unionists are already being rounded up tonight — should there be a trial?

ANNIE. It's happening tonight? But —

FARHED. Absolutely not. It's too risky.

ANNIE. Too risky? Surely you're not advocating preventive detention.

FARHED. A very good idea that has to be looked at in the days and weeks ahead.

ANNIE. What about the Bill of Rights?

DENA. Hello? Can someone say the name of that river in Egypt? Denial.

ANNIE. But the Constitution —

FARHED. Do you think this madman, or these madmen, care about the Constitution?

ANNIE. What is going on, this is crazy. What is wrong with you people. You can't seriously advocate suspending elections, rounding up foreign nationals, or people who dissent, or — *(As she bloviates,*

Scott [or guard] comes around, tasers her, then, when she's caught of guard, he handcuffs her hands behind her back. Other guard takes photos of her guard smiling as he tasers her.) Seventy years ago, Sinclair Lewis wrote a book called *It Can't Happen Here*, in which he outlined such a nightmarish scenario.

SCOTT. Seventy years ago?

ANNIE. Yes.

SCOTT. And in all that time, it hasn't happened. Has it. So, actually, he was right, It Can't Happen Here.

ANNIE. But it's happening. It's happening tonight!

SCOTT. See ya!!! *(Scott [or guard] pushes her off, now Dena moves to Farhed.)*

DENA. Farhed, you understand, no hard feelings here. *(Farhed offers his wrists, Dena helps him into an orange jumpsuit, then handcuffs him.)*

FARHED. Absolutely. The important thing is not to alarm people. To stay calm. Sensible precautions, lightweight clothing, plenty of fluids, seal and tape all windows doors and most of us will be just fine. *(Farhed keeps issuing his precautions as he too is pushed off-set as well.)*

DENA. Folks, what you're seeing here is happening live, and happening all over the country. For the protection of our democratic ways. The president will be speaking later today at a speech he was scheduled to deliver to the North Carolina Homemakers society, and he may touch on this subject.

SCOTT. If any contact can be made with him, or if he's able to land. In the meantime, don't touch that dial — we know where you live. Just kidding. But stay tuned. You're watching *Fear Network News*, America's News, for Real Americans. *(They high five.)*

End of Play

PROPERTY LIST

Handcuffs
Camera
Orange jumpsuits
Taser

SOUND EFFECTS

Newsroom background noise, starting low and ending loud
Words being spoken: "Fear. Terror. Death. Germs. Anthrax.
    Weapons. Explosion. Bombs. Death. Fear. Terror. Terror.
    Bomb."
Big monumental important hip musicic

PAY-PER-KILL

CHARACTERS

ROBIN JUSTICE — Fast-talking, cheery host of *Pay-Per-Kill.*

DENNIS TOM HOKAMP — 34-year-old white drifter.

RUDY GIULIANI — Former Republican Mayor of New York City.

HILLARY CLINTON — Bleeding heart Liberal Democrat.

SHAMUS HOVING — 19-year-old African American. Slow-witted.

"FATHER JOHN" — a model of false piety.

REPORTER — A young news hound.

SARAH ANNE — Dennis Tom Hokamp's fiancée. A simple woman who believes in God and TV.

SECOND REPORTER, "AL" — Another eager news hound.

BISHOP ELDER — Southern spokesman.

GOVERNOR MERVIN THOMPSON — Pandering politician.

JOSEPH HOVING — Shamus' brother.

PAY-PER-KILL

Music up: big-sporting-event-on-TV-fanfare. Lights up: on a TV press box studio. The kind of box constructed for coverage of a political convention, Monday Night Football, or, as in this case ...

ROBIN JUSTICE. *(Taking cue from an unseen director.)* Hey hey hey, America. It's Friday night. T.G.I.F. Thank God It's ... FRY-time. Yes sirree, the weekend is here and what kind of weekend would it be if you didn't start it out with your weekly, LIVE, PAY! PER! VIEW! EXECUTION! I'm your host, Robin Justice, and along with our whole PAY PER KILL/Court TV team, I'm happy to bring you another FRIDAY NIGHT LIVE AT THE DEATH CHAMBER.

All week long you've heard their stories, you've seen their crimes reenacted, and now you've got just a few minutes left to dial that 900 number at the bottom of the screen to sign on for tonight's show. It's $39.95, and we guarantee a killing. Live. Tonight — *(Lights up on two losers, in separate spaces.)* — one of these two men will die. Crime doesn't pay, and one of these men is going to pay the ultimate price for what he did. And you, the PAY PER KILL audience, will get to be ... the hangin' jury.

You've got ten seconds left, America, order now. *(Counts it down.)* Six, five, four, three, two OK — half the country has signed up, and the other half is freeloadin'. Next week, watch it on your own sets, folks. Heh heh. OK — it's time for the main event. Let's meet our Death Row Boys.

First, from Tallahassee, Florida, here for his second week in a row, the little boy who grew up to be quite a menace, Dennis Tom Hokamp, the CIRCLE K KILLER. *(Lights up brighter on Dennis Tom, an unshaven, 34-year-old white drifter. While the Host is a TV performer, Dennis — and all the other guests — are real people who, for a variety of tragic reasons, are now getting their fifteen minutes. They do not perform in a fake way.)*

ROBIN JUSTICE. Now Dennis —
DENNIS. *(Interrupting.)* Call me Tom.
ROBIN JUSTICE. O-kayyy. Tom, as you know, was convicted of robbing several Circle K convenience stores across America, particularly in the southwest. In the course of one or two of those robberies, well, Tom got a little trigger-happy. *(No reply.)*
ROBIN JUSTICE. Didn't you, Tom.
DENNIS. I swear I didn' shoot anyone.
ROBIN JUSTICE. Still claiming his innocence, all the way to death row.
DENNIS. The people I killed — that was killed, not that I'm admittin' to anything here — but they was mostly Arabs.
ROBIN JUSTICE. OK, good point, Tom. Most of them *were* Arabs. Or at any rate some sort of Third World immigrants. We do have some hidden camera tape *(Looks up at unseen monitor.)* but as Tom's lawyers have pointed out, it's kind of fuzzy, and the action takes place out of camera view *(Winces at something.)* ... for the most part. Now let's give a Pay-Per-Kill welcome to our two experts. First, you can love him, you can hate him, but you have to respect him ... MY Mayor and Presidential candidate, Rudolph Guiliani, and *(Sweet now.)* also this week's guest, you can love her, you can hate her, but you don't have to sleep with her husband, our former First Lady, Hillary Rodham Clinton. *(Lights up on Rudy and Hillary. Seated in swivel chairs. Wearing Pay-Per-Kill blazers.)* Whichever of these two America gets to know the least, is the one most likely to get to the White House. *(Hillary and Rudy force laughs. [Note: Hillary and Rudy are this season's Left/Right, He Says/She Says Couple. If the play is performed next year, please substitute the newest pair of Media Flavors of the Month.])*
RUDY. Good one, Robin. *(Now mimes holding a pistol at audience, or the convicts.)* BANG! ... Gotcha.
ROBIN JUSTICE. Your Honor, Hillary, what do you think of our first mad dog?
RUDY. Ah, ladies first, Ms. Clinton.
HILLARY. This is harder than might first be apparent. I see the defendant, Denni — I mean Thomas's point. The killing itself *does* take place off screen. And he's with a partner who was never caught. When the government is in a position of taking someone's life. It must be abso —
ROBIN JUSTICE. Hold on there, Hillary. Mr. Mayor?
RUDY. Thumbs down. He's a lowlife. It doesn't matter who the trigger man was. He was there. Force was used. An eye for an eye.

I say fry 'em. It'll be the best thing that ever happened to him. Maybe give him a chance to straighten himself out.

ROBIN JUSTICE. OK, folks — a split decision from our judges. Now it's time for you to be the judge. If you want to see Dennis Tom Hokamp go down, call 1-900-CIRCLE K. Your call will be recorded. Now let's move over to the other side of the death row tracks and let's meet nineteen-year-old Shamus Hoving, from Dewitt, Mississippi. Shamus — *(Lights on a poor, confused black kid.)* — tried to steal a car in a shopping mall. When the owner showed up, a young pregnant mother of one, a scuffle ensued, and she was shot to death.

SHAMUS. *(Kind of dim.)* She pull the gun. I'm ... I'm just really sorry about the whole thing. But I didn't kill her.

ROBIN JUSTICE. By the way, while trying to make his getaway, Shamus ran over her as well. Judges?

RUDY. This is not the sort of man you just lock up and throw away the key so three years from now he gets probation by some liberal judge and is back on the streets. He shot her in a mall — not in his own neighborhood. Not his own people. What he did to her could happen to any one of our wives. What reason is there for this man to go on living? At taxpayer expense.

ROBIN JUSTICE. All right, Rudy! Thumbs down twice tonight. Mrs. Clinton?

HILLARY. Well — from what I understand he ... he's not necessarily capable of understanding what he did. Um, mentally or emotionally. I know that he comes from a broken home and was —

ROBIN JUSTICE. Sounds like another split decision, it's gonna be a close one tonight, folks, I can feel it. Dial 1-900-MOM KILL or CIRCLE K. Now, I know a lot of you folks would be happy to see both of these mad dogs die tonight. The only way to put a value on human life is to kill people who don't. But in a civilized society, we all have to make choices, so get to your phones. And cast your votes. By the way, Tom, I understand you plan to get married next week.

DENNIS. Yes, I do, sir. The good Lord and the folks out there willing ...

ROBIN JUSTICE. We'll see ... Final seconds. Vote. Vote. Vote. You are the jury. And ... it's over, folks. And according to our ace statistician, Chip Sorrow — whew, not even close ... TOM! — *(This scares the living daylights out of Tom.)* — two weeks in a row, and you're still alive. We'll see you again next week. Maybe the third time will prove the charm. *(Winks at him.)*

DENNIS. Sure thing.

ROBIN JUSTICE. *(Turns now to Shamus.)* Barring a last-minute pardon, it looks like it's really over. *(Shamus doesn't say anything.)* How do you feel?

SHAMUS. I don' understand.

ROBIN JUSTICE. Are you sorry now? *(Shamus doesn't respond right away.)* Would you like to talk to a priest, or a man of the cloth?

SHAMUS. Yes, I think I would.

ROBIN JUSTICE. Great. While the Reverend makes his way up here, you might take this chance to choose which way you'd like to die.

SHAMUS. *(Not understanding.)* Pardon?

ROBIN JUSTICE. I don't think so. But you do have a choice between, now listen carefully, lethal injection, firing squad, poison gas, or electric chair.

SHAMUS. *(Nods along slowly.)* Uh, what was the third one?

ROBIN JUSTICE. Poison gas. Perhaps you'd like to talk it over with your preacher.

SHAMUS. No, I believe I'll go with the gas.

ROBIN JUSTICE. Gas it is. He's chosen the gas, ladies and gentlemen. Now, Shamus, while you sit down for a quick last meal-brought to you by McDonald's, you deserve a break today, so get out and get away to McDonald's — let's have Rudy tell our home viewers about the method of execution you have chosen.

RUDY. Well, as you and our fans know, gas is considered one of the slowest, or slower, ways to go. But perhaps one of the more peaceful. The convict is placed in a sealed room, a sodium cyanide pill is dropped into a canister, where it mixes with acid. Poison gas is produced, and a safe, sensible death ensues.

ROBIN JUSTICE. No fireworks tonight, then?

RUDY. No — I'm afraid it's a cowardly way out.

HILLARY. Actually, if I recall correctly, gas sometimes doesn't … well, there have been many cases where people have not received enough gas to die easily and they suffer in great pain. Convicted killer Carol Chessman told reporters he would blink if he felt pain *(Shamus hears this.)* from the gas, and he blinked throughout his ordeal. Even when it works right, it's still an inhumane —

ROBIN JUSTICE. *(Cutting her off.)* OK, Hillary, thank you. Gas — all in all — a sensible, humane way to go. Shamus, about done with that last meal? *(To audience.)* A McLean burger.

SHAMUS. Well, I … *(Meal is taken away. Shamus is led down*

Death Row. Robin Justice walks alongside.)
ROBIN JUSTICE. Folks, it's time for one final walk down that lonesome highway. *(Golf voice.)* Shamus, while you're on your way to the gas chamber, we know you'd like to have a few moments with our Father John ... just to confess, or to cleanse yourself. A few words between yourself, your minister, your god, and our home viewing audience ...
FATHER. Bless you, my son. *(They kneel with each other. Robin Justice stays standing.)*
ROBIN JUSTICE. *(Prompts.)* Shamus ...
SHAMUS.

 I want to tell my mommy I'm sorry for her
 She was my momma an I love her
 My papa he left me when I was just four
 I never seen him
 But I know if he's watching
 I don't know if he's out there watching
 like this
 but
 maybe. Why did you —
 I want my mom.

(Robin Justice signals Father to wrap it up. Father stands.)
ROBIN JUSTICE. *(To audience.)* Confession — it's good for the soul *(To Shamus.)* Feel better?
SHAMUS. *(Starts to sing, softly.)*

 I'M FRIGHTENED. I'M SORRY
 I'M READY TO DIE.
 JESUS HE LOVES ME
 MAMA DON'T CRY
 I'M SORRY I KILLED HER
 I'M SORRY SHE DIED

ROBIN JUSTICE. *(To audience.)* Just moments to go, folks. *(Shamus is led to the chamber as he continues singing.)*
SHAMUS.

 MY STOMACH IS ACHING,
 MY MOUTH HAS GONE DRY.
 I KNOW THAT I SHOT HER,
 I JUST DON'T KNOW WHY.
 JESUS IS WAITING
 MAMA DON'T CRY
 I'M SORRY, I'M SORRY

MAMA DON'T CRY

(He's in the chamber now. Doctor, guards attend to him.)
ROBIN JUSTICE. *(Repeating — not in song.)* "I'm sorry. I'm sorry. Mama don't cry." With those last words, convicted killer Shamus Hoving is now led into the gas chamber. As he undergoes some last-minute preparations, *(Show him being strapped in place, bolted in.)* let's go to the field. First to the home of Circle K killer Dennis Tom Hokamp's fiancée and family, where the feeling is:
REPORTER. One of relief, Robin. You can imagine the tension as the nation voted, and you can imagine the sense of relief when the tally came in. Now, of course, there is also a lingering anxiety.
ROBIN JUSTICE. Because he still has to come back next week?
REPORTER. That's right. *But,* if he makes it through a third week, his sentence will be commuted to life imprisonment. And with me now, the Circle K killer's fiancée, Sarah Anne. A good night for you?
SARAH ANNE. *(To camera.)* We're very happy. Of course, I'm sad for the Hoving boy, but it's either him or my Tommy, so I just thank the lord he heard our prayers tonight. And thank America for sparing Tommy. He never meant no harm.
REPORTER. And next week? I understand there's a little wedding planned.
SARAH ANNE. *(Beams.)* Yes … on Thursday. At the prison. They won't let him come out.
REPORTER. Do you hope for a long marriage?
SARAH ANNE. Yes, I do. I truly do. He's a good man and I think people, the more they get to know him, they can see that. I have faith. … I love you Tommy.
REPORTER. Robin …
ROBIN JUSTICE. If Tom does survive a third vote, he'll be the first man to escape Death Row since Pay-Per-Kill began. The odds don't look good. Now. How about the family of the Hoving boy? In Dewitt, Mississippi.
SECOND REPORTER. Well, there isn't much family left here, and few people remember him. Many people left when the mall opened up and Main Street was shuttered. His father, as he alluded to in his last final confession, left at an early age. His mother is currently in an institution. Still, Council Bishop Elder has agreed to speak for the people of Dewitt.
BISHOP ELDER. Well, we're not proud of what he has done. We jus' want people to know that sort of thing doesn't reflect on the

rest of us here. Mostly it's decent law-abiding people. And we all love your show, Robin.

SECOND REPORTER. There you have it: the feeling here — embarrassment, concern, and, frankly, a desire to just put this whole tragedy behind them.

ROBIN JUSTICE. *(Taking his cue.)* Can't blame them, Al. Glad to hear they're fans. To the state capitol with Governor Mervin Thompson. Governor — any chance for a last-minute pardon?

GOVERNOR. I do not think so.

ROBIN JUSTICE. Really?

GOVERNOR. I'm only sorry we can't fry the both of them tonight. The people of my state want justice. And I want you to know, tomorrow, every school child will see a videotape of tonight's broadcast, because this is how the children will learn.

ROBIN JUSTICE. Thank you, Governor. By the way — if your kids have wandered from the set, or fallen asleep, now would be a good time to wake them up, because we are one minute away from going live to the gas, and as the governor says — they need to learn right from wrong. As you can see, Shamus is in the chamber now, the doctors have examined him. He's been secured to his chair — we're just moments away. *(To his earpiece.)* What's that? Great. *(To audience.)* We have just found a half-brother of Shamus. We go now to Tacoma, Washington, where Joseph Hoving is standing by. Joseph … What do you think is going through your brother's mind right now?

JOSEPH. *(A little less dim.)* I never, you know, knew him. But I think. I think he look OK I think he'll take it like a man.

ROBIN JUSTICE. Shamus's half-brother, live from Tacoma. And we're live at the Death Chamber, where convicted mom murderer Shamus Hoving waits, strapped in, ready to meet his maker. The clock is ticking down. The Governor's phone is right here in case there's a last-minute change of plans. Five. Four. Three. *(Looks at phone — nothing.)* Two. Kill time! *(Sound of aerosol.)* The pellet has dropped, ladies and gentlemen. Let's just watch … *(The stage darkens. Only Shamus, in his chair, in dimmer and dimmer light. His breathing becomes labored. He starts to blink. First a little. Then a lot. Blackout.)*

End of Play

PROPERTY LIST

Hamburger on a plate
Straps on chair in gas chamber
Earpiece for TV host

SOUND EFFECTS

Aerosol can
Music: Big sports-event-on-TV fanfare

JUDAIC PARK

CHARACTERS

STEVEN SPIELBERG — Steven Spielberg.

BARRY — Chairman of the motion picture company.

BEN — Barry's son.

JANE — Movie executive. Dressed and trained to kill.

SCOTT — Movie executive. Dressed and trained to kill.

JUDAIC PARK

Steven Spielberg walks into the room. Barry, the Chairman, is on the phone. Scott and Jane, dressed and trained to kill, whisper. They see Steven. Love time. Arms out. Big hugs. Except from Scott.

JANE. Steven!
BARRY. Steven.
SCOTT. Steven.
STEVEN. Jane, Barry, Scott. *(Ben, the young, eager one, gets ignored.)*
BEN. Mister Steven E.T. Jurassic Fucking Park Spielberg. *(Everyone looks at Ben. He has no idea he's done anything wrong.)*
SCOTT. Steven, I don't know if you've met Barry's son, Ben — *(Ben lunges to shake hands.)*
BEN. I loved *1941*, let me —
SCOTT. *(Cutting him off.)* Get you anything you'd like to drink.
STEVEN. I'm fine.
BARRY. Perrier?
JANE. D.C.?
BEN. Reese's Pieces? *(They look at him.)*
STEVEN. I'm fine.
BARRY. Get Steven some Evian. *(Ben vanishes. To Steven:)* Bright boy. Loves your work.
SCOTT. So — *Schindler's List.*
STEVEN. *Schindler's List.*
JANE. *What* a great story.
STEVEN. Well, it's not a story. It's based on a true holocaust — and it's just a first draft.
BARRY. Listen to him. Would you listen to him?
SCOTT. First draft. Nothing you write could ever be a first draft.
STEVEN. I didn't actually write — *(Ben rushes in faster than any assistant in history.)*
BARRY. *(To Steven.)* STOP —
BEN. No Evian. I got Crystal Geyser, or Badoit. Or Poland —

75

(Barry takes the bottles from him. Snaps his fingers. Ben sits.)
BARRY. *(To Ben.)* SIT. *(Ben sits.)* Steven, please, let me just say, I —
SCOTT. *WE* —
JANE. *All* of us —
BARRY, JANE, and SCOTT. *LOVE* THE SCRIPT.
STEVEN. Really?
SCOTT. Absolutely.
JANE. Fantastic.
STEVEN. Because I was — I'll be honest, it's a little different than my other stuff.
BARRY. A little?
SCOTT. Unrecognizable.
BARRY. *(Quickly.)* But it's great.
JANE. A-list.
SCOTT. Abso-fucking-lutely. We're sniffing Oscars on this one.
STEVEN. Now don't start getting —
BARRY. No. No. What did I say, Ben, when I read this? What did I say. *(Ben has spaced out, staring at Steven.)* Ben!
BEN. Oh ah ... *(Reading Barry's lips.)* Ossss-cars. Right, Oscars. Oscars. Right?
BARRY. I said — Oscars for Oskar. Get it? Oskar Schindler? Oscar? Get it?
STEVEN. That's very good. *(Everyone laughs.)* But — I don't want to get anyone's hopes up. Least of all mine. Besides — it's kind of — new territory for me — and I'm just grateful to have your support.
SCOTT. Support?
JANE. Support.
BARRY. Support — Steven — you have our ... admiration.
JANE. Admiration? Ad*ulation.*
SCOTT. Adulation? Adulation? *(He's thinking.)* Awe. Fucking *Awe.*
BARRY. Awe? Awe. Take your pants down Steven. I want to kiss your ass.
SCOTT. Me too.
STEVEN. It's not really neccesar —
JANE. Drop trou, S. Man.
STEVEN. Well, just this once — why not? *(He starts to drop his pants.)*
BEN. I'll suck your cock. *(Everyone looks at Ben. Steven starts to zip up.)* What?
STEVEN. Some other time. So — ahh — that's it? No notes?
BARRY. I wouldn't change a word.

SCOTT. Not word one.

STEVEN. GREAT. That is great. So I'll have my people get in touch with your people — schedule, budget, how we're going to do the black and white.

SCOTT. Ahh. Black and white. That ... that's something. Ah — isn't black and white kind of ... old.

STEVEN. Old?

BARRY. You know — dated.

JANE. It's kind of ... *down* too. I mean — we don't want people to think we couldn't afford color for like, only the most important film director in the world.

BEN. Mister Steven Spielberg himself. *(Everyone looks at Ben.)*

STEVEN. I don't think they'd think that. I just — I'm going for kind of a documentary, non-sensationalist feel —

JANE. Oh absolutely.

SCOTT. Of course —

BARRY. It's just ... ahh ... think about you know ... maybe using color to get that same feel but ... *(To anyone.)* help me out here ...

JANE. But with ... color.

STEVEN. Use color to get the black and white feel?

BARRY. Exactly.

SCOTT. Listen to him. A genius.

STEVEN. BUT —

BARRY. NO BUTS about it, you're a genius Steven. Color to get that black and white feel. I love it. It's less down.

JANE. Much.

SCOTT. You know — speaking of ... the whole *(Makes quote marks in air.)* "*down* issue."

STEVEN. Well — wait a minute — it is about the holocaust.

BARRY. I know, I know, Steven — a movie like this has to have its down moments —

JANE. But Scott was wondering —

SCOTT. All of us —

BARRY. The ending — when the Jews are freed — that has such a *nice* feeling to it —

SCOTT. Very nice —

BARRY. We were wondering — and you know best here —

JANE. But ... couldn't we have a little bit more of that *UP* feeling — throughout the film.

STEVEN. *(Confused.)* I'm sorry — I don't see what you're getting at it.

SCOTT. STEVE — This is just — I'm just talking out loud here, but — do the Jews have to be … prisoners *throughout* the story.

JANE. I mean — they're such *victims.*

BARRY. With all due respect, Steven — and believe me — I'm in fucking awe of your talent —

SCOTT. We all are.

BARRY. But … and this may be crazy — but … does this movie have to be about — Jews?

STEVEN. I don't believe I'm hearing —

SCOTT. Now Steven — we all know you've worked hard on this. You're very close to the script. But we've worked hard too — hear us out a little.

BEN. Couldn't Schindler free … a whale? *(Steven looks at Ben. Everyone else kind of likes the idea.)*

STEVEN. No. No. No. Schindler couldn't free a whale.

JANE. How about an alien? I mean — an *alien* alien. Not a Mexican — but, you know, a cute one. From outer space.

STEVEN. I don't think you understand.

JANE. *(Furious now.)* I don't think *you* understand.

BARRY. WAIT A MINUTE. WAIT A MINUTE. I got it. Let's face it — we all know the script is too down — Steven — you know it. We know it. But what if — forget Schindler for a second — what if … the Dinosaurs freed your Jews. OK?

STEVEN. They're not *my* Jews, for Crissakes.

BARRY. *But* — instead of Schindler — who is basically an unattractive guy — I think we can all agree —

SCOTT. *(Taking his cue.)* He's not very … *sympathetic.*

BEN. *(Piling on now.)* I'll say.

JANE. He smokes.

BARRY. And drinks. So forget him —

STEVEN. *Schindler?* You don't have a movie —

SCOTT. Steven — I think we all know when we have a movie. When we have a hero who smokes, who saves a bunch of skinny faceless victims with accents and bad hair, we don't have a movie. When we have sharks or dinosaurs attacking the goyim, or the goyim attacking *one* cute extraterrestrial *then* we have a movie.

BARRY. May I finish here? MAY I FINISH. What if — instead of this white trash Sch*im*ler—who sounds Jewish anyway —

STEVEN. SCHINDLER is not Jewish.

BARRY. Don't give me that. The man's a Jew. What if — hear me out — either the dinosaurs save one cute Jew — like an Amy Irving

type, for example — *(Everyone winces at this reference.)*
BEN. I like her.
STEVEN. NO.
BARRY. *OR.* OR — and this is another way — what if — you want this Schundler. What if — say — it's later in the war — the Nazis have won —
STEVEN. The Nazi's *didn't* win —
SCOTT. Mr. History all of a sudden. You know how many people have been killed by sharks on the east coast since the Nazis won World War Two? Do you? Tell him:
JANE. Zero.
SCOTT. That's right — Zippo. So — don't tell me about history Mr. Da-duh Da-duh. We're talking movie.
BARRY. Steven — if I may — and this is I think a way to keep a lot of what brought you to the project —
JANE. All of us —
BARRY. What if — the Nazis have won. There are no Jews left — anywhere. Except that a mad scientist —
SCOTT. A Mengele type — say we get Chris Lloyd.
JANE. And Kathleen Turner can play his wife.
BARRY. Great idea — she's very good with accents. The two of them — open sort of a recreation park — a game park — they've saved some of — I don't know — genetic material — help me out —
JANE. DNA!
BARRY. DNA — and they've grown these really BIG JEWS. BIG JEWS. You with me?
STEVEN. I'm listening. Big Jews.
SCOTT. Enormous.
BARRY. And these Jews are kept in the park — like your camps — maybe a little more up — but very similar —
STEVEN. They're not *my* camps.
BEN. Hear my dad out. He's trying to help.
BARRY. And Schindler —
SCOTT. Maybe we change his name — Jones. Switzerland Jones —
BARRY. He breaks into this ... Schindler's Park call it for now, no wait — *JUDAIC PARK.* Better. This *JUDAIC PARK* — and he frees the BIG JEWS.
JANE. I love this.
BARRY and BEN. I'm getting chills.
STEVEN. I don't think —
SCOTT. Steven — you don't have to answer right away. It proba-

79

bly seems like a big change — it's not — but it probably seems big.
BARRY. You get to keep your Jews — there's less of them, but they are bigger. You keep Schindler — it seems to us —
JANE. Absolutely.
SCOTT. Very much like the movie you were trying to make, before you got sidetracked with all that history downer stuff.
BARRY. At the end — and this is something only you can do Steven — if the Big Jews are freed — and they make their escape — what if they got on bicycles — and biked out of the camp — into the sky silhouetted against a full moon. *(Ben starts to cry.)*
SCOTT. Look at the boy — he's crying. Tears Steven.
BARRY. A heck of a lot more tears than you'll get with your little black and white museum piece.
JANE. I'm crying too. *(She isn't. She's faking. Now Barry starts to sob.)*
SCOTT. Steven — trust us. Black and white, faceless victims — the people can stay home and watch it on A&E — for free. No parking. No sitter. This — Big Jews escaping *JUDAIC PARK* on Big Bikes — this is a *movie*.
STEVEN. *(Wavering.)* I kind of wanted to do something ... different. *(Scott starts to walk Steven out of the room.)*
BARRY. Steven — just think about it. You don't have to say yes right away. And I know you don't care about merchandising — but that's another factor. Think about it. Sleep on it. Talk it over with your people. We're always here for you. *(Jane and Scott watch Steven go. They exchange high fives.)* Who's next?

End of Play

PROPERTY LIST

Phone

Three bottles of water, three different brands (Evian, Crystal
    Geyser, Badoit, Poland Springs)

WHAT I DID WRONG

CHARACTER

WOMAN

WHAT I DID WRONG

She sits alone in her car, parked at the water's edge. Smoking a cigarette.

WOMAN. He shouldn't have left me. If he hadn't left me I'd know what to do.

I would do what he wanted.

Or rather, I would do what I guess he wanted. Which was not necessarily what he *really* wanted. He never really knew what he wanted. This drove me crazy. Twice.

While I was with him, and while he was leaving me.

No. Most of the time he didn't know what he wanted. And if he did know, he wouldn't say. And so, all I had to do, was figure out what he wanted, despite what he'd say, or not say, then, once I'd figured it out, I'd do it.

And resent him.

Because he never even noticed how hard I was working.

Divining his needs.

He only noticed if I screwed up. If I gave him something he didn't want. Or not enough of what he did want. Or too much. Then he'd notice. If I made the wrong guess, he'd notice. If I guessed right, he'd resent it.

He'd resent me for guessing right. For meeting his unspoken, unknown to himself needs. When I got on a roll, and really took care of him, he'd sleep with her. Just to let me know I wasn't going to trick him into becoming dependent on me.

But he never left. All that time I was working to please him, or failing to please him, or upsetting him by pleasing him, he always came home. In all that time he never left.

What did me in, what ruined it, was the day — and I hate myself for this — the day I needed something.

The day I said, I need help, I'm in trouble here. I need you. That was the day he left. Casually. As if he were going down to the corner for a pack of cigarettes.

And he never came back.

End of Play

PROPERTY LIST

Cigarette

NORM-ANON

CHARACTERS

Three happy, well-adjusted people:

JUDY RODGERS

BOB ALLEN, JR.

ANNIE ROSS

NORM-ANON

Onstage, three happy, well-adjusted people.

JUDY. Hi, my name is Judy Rodgers.

BOB. Hi, I'm Bob Allen, Junior.

ANNIE. And I'm Annie Ross. And though we may look different ...

BOB. All three of us have something in common: a secret about our past.

JUDY. A secret that, as we grew older, kept us isolated from others. You see, all three of us are:

ALL. Adult Children of Normal Parents.

JUDY. For years I denied it. When my friends talked about their dysfunctional homes, and codependent parents, I tried to mix in. I pretended that my childhood had also been one of constant instability and emotional trauma. The truth was, I was living a lie. The truth is, my parents were normal. And so was I.

ANNIE. In college, my roommate — Sylvia, was having a hard time of it. She stayed inside our dorm room, on the floor, for two weeks, listening to Aimee Mann CD's. One day I asked her to come out for a walk with me.

"I can't," she said. "I'm depressed."

"Depressed," I asked. "What's that?"

You see, I had never heard the word, and I had no idea what she was talking about. I felt so embarrassed.

BOB. I can relate to what Annie ... Ross, is saying. At work I used to wonder, am I the only one here not subject to mood swings, or obsessive compulsive behavior. I didn't feel guilty about it, or superior — I mean, guilt or shame or grandiosity never really solve anything. And we all have to do the best we can with what we've been given, but sometimes I did wonder, just for a little while ... AM I the only one? I enjoyed life, and still do. But sometimes not so often, not for any length of time, I felt a little ... alone.

Until I found NORM-ANON.

JUDY. Yes, all three of us are grateful members of Norm-Anon.

Norm-Anon: a support group for happy people. Healthy people who grew up in clean, well-lit homes.

There aren't many of us.

ANNIE. And sometimes it helps to get together.

BOB. To talk about … what it was like, coming from those homes. How great the holidays were.

JUDY. How much we miss Mom 'n' Dad.

ANNIE. And Gran'pa.

BOB. And the girl, or fella, next door.

JUDY. Once a week or so, we get together, to talk about feelings. Of course, we know feelings aren't facts. And feelings, good or bad, pass. And we all know, without question, really, that everything always works out for the best. Still, on those days when everything isn't coming up roses, it's good to get together with people who understand.

BOB. Right now, you may be asking, how do I know if I'm an adult child of normal parents?

ANNIE. Well, if you have to ask, you're probably not. But, we do have a short handy checklist, that can help you decide: Ask yourself the following questions:

JUDY. Do you find yourself genuinely happy for the success of family or friends?

BOB. Do anniversaries and holidays fill you with a sense of joy?

ANNIE. Do you have twenty/twenty vision. A perfect dental history. And good skin?

JUDY. Do you often find yourself telling the truth, when a lie would do just as well.

BOB. If you answered yes to any or one of these questions, it's a good bet — not that any of us likes to bet — that you're one of us. An adult child of normal parents —

If you're tired of being with people who act out, or feel sorry for themselves, or need to learn things you knew when you were four, maybe it's time you tried Norm-Anon.

JUDY. Call us.

ANNIE. We're all in the book.

BOB. Thanks.

JUDY. C'mon guys, let's go get some sodas.

ALL. Bye for now.

End of Play

THE MORNING
AFTER SHOW

CHARACTERS

PETER DARTWELL — Game-show host.

TOD — California dude.

TONY — Heavy-set, working-class guy.

KENT — Tall, good-looking preppy.

RACHEL — Sexy, All-American Valley girl.

TRACEY — A pragmatist. Does the best she can with what she's got.

ELAINE — Slightly frumpy.

Optional: Dancer 1, Dancer 2

THE MORNING AFTER SHOW

A cutsie-wootsie game show/bedroom set. Two beds form a V, with a host's chair at the point. Upstage are three doors, each of which leads to an unseen bedroom. Music — perhaps "Come Fly with Me" — starts the show.* Our smarmy, slick, but kind of likable host, Peter, bounds out to center stage as crowd goes wild. (Note: The crowd has been pumped full of testosterone. At every hint of a sexual innuendo, they go wild. Football fans at the Super-Orgy.)

PETER.   Hello hello. Wake up! Rise and shine America. Gooooooooood Morning everyone — it's time once again foooooor: *The Morning After! (Down front. Big grin on his face.)* The only TV show that dares to go behind bedroom doors, under the covers, and even ... between the sheets ... *The Morning After. (The host, and all guests, apparently get paid every time they mention the title:* The Morning After.*)* To find out just what happened ... the night before. I'm your host, Peter Dartwell, live from fabulous Lake Tahoe, Nevada, where last night three lovely ladies — one look at them and let's just say you don't need a chairlift, huh ho — and three of our studly guys got a chance to dine, dance, pitch a little woo, and maybe, just maybe, get a little night skiing in. Now it's time to find out who did what to whom, how hard, and how often. First, let's bond with our studs ... *(Out come the boys. Tod, a California surf's up dude, has thrown on shorts and a T-shirt. Tony, a heavy-set, working-class guy, wears a Playboy robe. Kent, tall and good-looking, is prepped out in chinos, blue blazer and a button-down shirt.)*
TOD.   Hey dudes. Loco-motion.
TONY.   Tell me about it.
KENT.   *(Sheepish.)* Hi, guys. *(Offers his hand to Tony. Tony sniffs his own finger, then offers Kent a sniff.)*
TONY.   Get a whiff.

95

PETER. OK. Looks like none of our stud men are any the worse for wear. *(Teasing.)* Tod, you and — what was her name again? —
TOD. *(Stumped.)* You mean … her name?
PETER. *(To audience.)* Tod: nice house, but the attic is empty.
TOD. Oh. Right. OK. *(To Peter.)* Rachel?
PETER. Rachel ended up in the Honeymoon Suite. How'd you talk her into the sheets?
TOD. OK. I said, Hi, I'm Tod, I'm your waiter. Oh wait, I said, My name is Tod and if, you know, we don't move soon, someone else is gonna grab that suite so … it might as well, you know, be us. And she was like, totally cool about it.
PETER. OK. Tod, the straight ahead approach. Sometimes it works. Once you got her across the threshold, what happened?
TOD. You know … um … we made love.
PETER. Oh … would you say she was hot to trot, a mudder, or did she come up lame?
TOD. Oh wow — well, the first time, definitely hot to trot. Definitely. The second time, well. It was, you know …
PETER. A slippery track?
TOD. Well, um —
PETER. That's OK, we get the idea. Tony. How 'bout your night?
TONY. First of all, let me just say — you guys get some terrific babes on this show. I mean: Grade A. Am I right?
TOD. PRIMO.
KENT. They were all lovely.
TONY. "Lovely." Get a load of this guy. But anyway, I went for um …
PETER. *(Helping.)* Tracey.
TONY. *(Makes a little pistol finger.)* Right. Tracey because, you know, Tod had already moved on the blonde so that's life … but Tracey was a good girl. She was definitely hot to trot. Like you say. You know — a lot of laughs. And uh … hot.
PETER. OK, Tony — and orgasms? Any luck there?
TONY. Oh yeah. I don't know. I'd say like … *(Looks at the other guys.)* forty … fifty, somewhere in there.
PETER. We're talking real ones here, Tony. Tod?
TOD. Just one *(Crowd disappointed.)* … but it was like a long one. Like six or seven hours, I'd say.
PETER. OK. Kent — pretty tough competition here. Can you cut it?
KENT. I'm a little more old-fashioned than the other guys here.

PETER. Uh-oh. Katie bar the door. A shut-out. Zippo. Air ball.

TOD AND TONY. AIR-BAAAAL. Air-baaalll. Air-baaaaal.

KENT. *(He looks at them with disdain.)* Well, that's not exactly correct. I just ... we needed time to get to know each other. I told her about my family. And school.

PETER. The "let her get to know you slow and natural" approach?

KENT. I guess so.

PETER. Did it work? *(Kent doesn't answer. Prodding:)* What happened when you went ... behind the green door?

KENT. *(Begrudgingly spills it.)* Well, she was ... she was uninhibited.

PETER. Could you be a little more specific?

KENT. She was like — a different person. Scratching and thrashing. She definitely goes wild when she gets between the sheets.

PETER. And what did you do?

KENT. I grabbed on tight and held on for the ride.

PETER. Whew. Sssss. Three hot to trots, and from the looks of it *(Points to Kent's cheek.)* one of 'em scratched early as well. A hot time in Tahoe, according to the fellas. But now it's time for the ladies to tell us which of our wildmen are blowing smoke, and which one really was ... the biggest stud ... *(The ladies are brought in and seated on the bed opposite the men. Rachel looks fresh, glowing, perky. Tracey has tried to get her self together, but she is really hung over. Her hair is still a mess. She clutches a cup of coffee. Next to her is Elaine. She seems oddly detached. In her own world.)*

PETER. OK, let's say hello to our lovely ladies. *(Note: Peter's manner with the women is much more solicitous, "concerned" and understanding than when he's locker-rooming it up with the guys. When he says lines like "our lovely ladies," he says them with a very sincere veneer of chivalry and appreciation.)* ... and let's find out how they're feeling the morning after, and who will win our dream weekend for two. Rachel — I almost didn't recognize you without the sheet around you.

RACHEL. Oh stop, silly. *(She's dressed in a short skirt and tight blouse. Put together in a squeaky-clean California way. Tracey tries for the same effect, with a lot less success. Elaine is kind of covered up and frumpy.)*

PETER. No, seriously — you ended up in the Honeymoon suite, would you care to tell us how Tod "suite"-talked you? Did he play you like a violin, lie like a rug, or let his fingers do the talking?

RACHEL. I think we just decided — heck, go for it. We wanted to have something to talk about, the morning after. *(Bells ring, indicating a correct answer.)*

PETER. OK, they both just went for it … *(He tosses each of them a ridiculous stick-on ribbon. Evidently they've garnered a point or something.)* And, once you went for it … how did it go …

RACHEL. *(Shy.)* Well, it was very romantic.

PETER. OK. Let me help you out here. Would you say, overall, your date was a Quick Draw McGraw, a Johnny Come Lately …

TONY. *(Cutting in.)* A Speedy Gonzalez … ha ha.

PETER. We'll get to you in a second, Speedy. *(Back to Rachel.)* Excuse him. Or somewhere in between.

RACHEL. Um *(Very demure.)* well, the first time, the second time, or the … *(Sound: Ding ding ding.)*

PETER. *(Tossing a condom bouquet.)* Oh, to be young and in lust. Now a toss-up question: We asked the guys how many orgasms you each had last night, and one of these Playboys over here told us — "somewhere between forty and fifty." Ladies.

RACHEL and TRACEY. *(Together.)* Tony. *(Sound: Ding ding ding. Tony all but prances.)*

PETER. You're right. Tony said it. Now Tracey, I can see how you might know, but Rachel — are the walls *that* thin?

RACHEL. *(Blushing.)* Nooooo. It just sounds like something Tony would say.

TRACEY. Yeah. He's, you know. A bullshit artist.

PETER. Are you saying you didn't have forty orgasms?

TRACEY. Get outta here. I mean, please. Tony, how could you say that?

PETER. Tony, how *could* you say that? Tracey — how many did you have?

TRACEY. I don't remember.

TONY. Whad I tell ya.

PETER. What do you remember, Tracey?

TRACEY. Well, we were both pretty drunk. Cuervo. You know, I told him I was feeling pretty sick and he was real nice about it, and he took me upstairs to his room …

PETER. NICE one, Tony.

TONY. Whatever it takes …

TRACEY. And then we like fooled around a little but I got sick on him so we stopped and then he took a shower and we tried to mess around a little more but he was pretty drunk too and so he couldn't really you know …

PETER. No, I *don't* know. What?

TRACEY. Perform. So he gets mad and I told him no big d, it

happens. Then he gets all weird and everything and says he's going for a walk. I think he went to the casino.

PETER. Judges? *(No ding ding ding.)* OK, the two stories don't quite match up. Tony?

TONY. Look. She liked it last night. Big. What can I say, she was, she was a whore. No offense, but a real whore. If she doesn't want people to know — hey, I know what happened. And she knows. I'm sorry to say this, because you know, she's a nice girl and everything, but she's a lying whore.

TRACEY. He has like, the littlest peter.

PETER. *(Cutting this one off.)* OK, right now, Tod and Rachel are in the lead, but things can change fast on the morning after. Fellas, we next asked the ladies to tell us what happened last night, between the sheets. One of them told us *(Reads from card in an over-the-top salacious manner.)* "He threw me on the bed and did ... *unspeakable* things to me" *(Crowd goes wild.)* "over and over." *(All three guys jump in.)*

TOD, TONY, and KENT. Gotta be me. That's me. Here you go.

PETER. Hold on there, fellas, put it back in your pants, 'cause there's more ... *(Reading again, this time in a sultry Marilyn Monroe voice.)* "I asked him to ... " *(Mouths this next word.)* "stop" *(Leering now.)* "but he wouldn't" *(Whisper.)* "stop." *(Crowd really goes wild. As do the guys.)*

TOD, TONY, and KENT. Definitely me. It sounds like Elaine and me.

PETER. OK, a three-way tie. Ladies. Help us out. Who's telling the truth? *(Tracey and Rachel do a To-Tell-the-Truth, you stand/I stand bit of shtick. After a few false stands, they both sit. Elaine sits in her own world.)* Tracey ... Rachel — any unspeakable things?

RACHEL and TRACEY. *(Together.)* Nooooo.

PETER. OK then — Elaine and Kent. Yow. *(Sound: Ding ding ding. Peter throws Kent a right-answer ribbon. Elaine sits there.)* Elaine, getting a little ... bashful the morning after? Was he that unspeakable?

ELAINE. *(Halting.)* It wasn't like that.

PETER. OK, then, did he do, *speakable* things?

ELAINE. No.

PETER. *(To the guys.)* Isn't it funny how they all turn sheepish, the morning after?

ELAINE. He ... I. I didn't want him to. I told him to stop ...

PETER. *(Picking it up, and filling in the punch line.)* but he wouldn't ... STOP!!! Right again, Kent. *(Sound: Ding ding ding. Another ribbon.)*

ELAINE. No. I meant. Stop. I said, "Don't. Please."

TONY. *(Laughing.)* Don't. Stop. Don't stop. *(Elaine starts to cry.)*

PETER. Uh oh, wait a minute. She's crying now, Tony. Nice one. Mr. Sensitive. *(To Elaine.)* What's the problem, honey … Kent got your tongue?

ELAINE. I was … raped.

KENT. Oh jesus.

ELAINE. Kent … raped me … *(She starts to cry.)*

TONY. Women.

TRACEY. Shut up.

PETER. Hey hey folks, simmer down. Elaine, you know the rules here on *The Morning After*. Rape is a heinous charge, one that we take very seriously. Are you sure there hasn't been some misunderstanding?

ELAINE. He raped me.

PETER. OK, OK. No reason to get upset. Every so often a couple wakes up on the morning after and can't seem to agree on what happened the night before. I, and the entire staff of *The Morning After*, know — there is nothing funny at all about Date Rape; when a charge is made, the game clock is put on hold until that charge can be resolved. which means … *(Peter hands Elaine a large blue dot on a stick. Now he stands, moves downstage, and beckons.)*

KENT. Oh for crissakes. I knew she was a wacko.

PETER. Kent, Elaine, come on down here for the He Said, She Said, Reasonable Doubt Rape Lightning Round — where anything can happen and the scores can really change.

TONY. *(As Kent stands.)* Go get her, man. *(He high-fives him. Elaine sits. Still.)*

PETER. Elaine, excuse me, Alleged Victim, come on down and tell us your story. *(He goes and gets her. Tries to get her to hold the dot in front of her face. Chairs appear for a Siskel-Ebert style confront.)*

ELAINE. It's not a story.

PETER. Of course it's not. No one said it was. Why don't you hold that little fella up *(Shows her how to hold the dot.)* and tell us your story.

ELAINE. It's not a story. It's true. Why don't you believe —

PETER. Hold on there, little lady, no one's even attacking you yet. Just try, take a deep breath. There. Now, in your own words, tell us what happened last night. After you took him to your room.

ELAINE. I didn't take him to my room.

PETER. Oh? But isn't that where the incident allegedly took place?

ELAINE. Yes. *(Tony vocalizes a buzzer sound.)*

TONY. Inconsistency.

PETER. Hey hey — Tony knows the rules. Elaine, just who *did* you take to your room?

ELAINE. No one. I ... I guess I had a little of that ... punch stuff. And I wasn't feeling so good. After dinner I danced a little. But I didn't really hit it off with any of the guys — I mean, I liked them OK, but —

PETER. No magic in the air.

ELAINE. *(Looks at him, tries to ignore his hostitude.)* So I ... you know ... I just thought I'd turn in early, to the girl's dorm. Maybe read a book.

PETER. *(Yawns.)* And that's when this heinous event occurred.

ELAINE. No. I guess I fell asleep. And then, later on — there was a knock on the door.

PETER. What time was this?

ELAINE. I ... I don't know. But I, you know, I figured it was one of the girls, you know, maybe locked out or something.

PETER. *(To the girls.)* Were any of you locked out? *(They shake their heads.)*

TRACEY and RACHEL. Noooo.

TONY. *(Inconsistency buzzer.)* There's another one.

PETER. Tony — a quick trigger. Now, you got to the door and ...

ELAINE. Ken was there.

PETER. Ken, or Kent?

ELAINE. Him. And —

PETER. You let him into your room ... *(She starts to cry again.)*

ELAINE. Yes. Not at first. But he said ...

PETER. Quickly, had you danced with him at all, earlier?

ELAINE. I think so. He seemed nice.

PETER. So you let him in.

ELAINE. Well — I didn't think it was, you know ... He told me the honeymoon suite was full, and the boys' dorm was ... being used. And he said he just wanted to crash. He was very tired. But I told him, you know, I didn't think it was a good idea, because ... I don't know.

PETER. And that's when this heinous crime occurred.

ELAINE. Well ... I told him, you know, I didn't want to do anything. That I was tired and just wanted to sleep. And he said, he was tired, too. And he just wanted to sleep.

PETER. Nice one, Kent.

ELAINE. And he made a joke. He said it looked like the two of us wouldn't have too much to say ... the morning after. *(Sound: Ding ding. Peter tosses her a prize. She cries.)*

PETER. So far, he sounds kind of sweet.

ELAINE. That's why I figured it was OK. I mean, he talked about his family and his school. I felt I could trust him.

PETER. Why is it always the trustworthy ones, ladies and gentlemen? Go on.

ELAINE. And I went back to my bed ...

PETER. After letting him in.

ELAINE. But I didn't want him to ... then all of a sudden he was on top of me, he threw me on the bed and he ...

PETER. DID UNSPEAKABLE THINGS TO YOU!

ELAINE. *(Crying.)* Yes.

PETER. And you told him to STOP! But he wouldn't ... *(Mike to audience.)*

AUDIENCE and OTHERS. STOP!

PETER. OK. Sounds awful. What happened next?

ELAINE. I don't know.

PETER. Did you struggle? Scream?

ELAINE. Yes. Yes.

PETER. *(Picking up pace.)* Where was your right arm?

ELAINE. He pinned it. Both of my arms.

TONY. Then how did you struggle? *(Mimics sound of the buzzer.)*

ELAINE. I don't know. I ... I ...

PETER. Kenny, how could you? *(Kent makes a "crazy" gesture. Solemn:)* And when it was over?

ELAINE. He said ... he said — well, this should give us a story for the morning after. *(Sound: Ding ding ding.)*

PETER. He did? Cruel stuff.

ELAINE. He ... he said if I said anything ... he would just tell everyone I I I liked it rough ... *(Breaks down in tears.)*

PETER. Folks, what an awful story. And believe me, if a word of it is true, not that we are doubting our Alleged Victim, here, but if she hasn't made this up, or fantasized it, let me assure you, Kent will not be eligible for our grand prize. Kent, you've heard these sick sick charges. What, if anything, can you say to defend yourself?

KENT. I just want to say — this is very troubling. I don't want to, you know — hurt her feelings, but I just don't know how to defend myself against this.

PETER. Try.

KENT. Elaine and I … *(Buzzer.)* I'm sorry, the Alleged Victim and I — you know, we had partied. We danced. Drank a little. She was kind of forward.

PETER. Did she rape you, Kent? Ha ha.

KENT. Well, I mean. Frankly she wasn't my type. I like *(Turns to Rachel.)* Rachel, but *(Rachel smiles back.)* you know — I kind of missed the boat on her, and even Tracey, so I danced with her, when she asked me …

PETER. She asked you?

KENT. Well, yeah. She was kind of forward in general. I'm kind of embarrassed saying this, but … when we were dancing, she whispered something … she said, "Everyone else has already paired up. You don't want to strike out on *The Morning After.*" *(Sound: Ding ding ding.)*

PETER. OK! And she invited *you* to the girls' dorm?

KENT. No, no. She said, "I'm going to go upstairs now … and I'm going to leave the door unlocked. What I want you to do is … " I feel embarrassed again … "Wait until I've gone to bed, then sneak upstairs, knock on the door, I'll let you in like you're just going to sleep, then I want you to throw me on the bed and" this was her own words here, "do unspeakable things to me."

PETER. Whoa! Steamy stuff! *(Catches himself.)* If true. and what did you say?

KENT. Well, I felt awkward. I didn't want to hurt her feelings. She said it was a big fantasy of hers. And I figured, you know, at least it would be a story for *The Morning After. (Sound: Ding ding ding.)*

PETER. Ah huh. *(Excited.)*

KENT. So I had a couple of drinks at the bar. Waiting. Then I snuck up to her room and did what she told me.

PETER. Wow.

KENT. It was hot. I threw her down like she said, and um, I mean, she just went wild.

PETER. "She just went wild." Elaine, I'm sorry, Alleged Victim, any rebuttal?

ELAINE. How can he? That's what happened, but it's not what happened. He's making it up. I didn't want him to …

PETER. Anybody follow that? No. Just checking. So Kent, you're saying, her description is correct, but that she *wanted* it?

KENT. Yeah, I guess so. *(Laugh.)* Crazy, huh?

PETER. And Elaine, you're holding to your version … *(Turns to the others.)* Folks …

TONY. I got a lot of inconsistencies here. In her story.

RACHEL. I do, too. She says she told him to stop, but he wouldn't stop.

PETER. Ah huh.

RACHEL. So that's inconsistent.

PETER. OK.

RACHEL. Also, why did she let him into the room if she knew he was going to rape her. I don't buy that.

ELAINE. I didn't know.

TONY. So what are you saying? You didn't know, but now you know? That's inconsistent.

RACHEL. He's very cute. I don't see why someone so handsome would need to rape someone.

PETER. OK, all good points. Did anyone hear any screaming?

TONY. In my room, heh heh heh.

TRACEY. You f'en liar. That's another thing. I see how on this show anyone can come on and just make up a story and, you know, how do we know she isn't just making this up?

ELAINE. Why would I make it up?

TRACEY. You tell me, sweetheart.

PETER. Tod, any thoughts?

TOD. Ah … yuh.

PETER. OK, so basically, it boils down to his word against hers …

TRACEY. His story, you know, collaborates with hers, but hers has a lot of inconsistencies.

RACHEL. And why would he do this if he knew she was going to tell everyone the morning after? *(Sound: Ding ding ding.)*

PETER. Wow — it sounds like there's a lot of reasonable doubt.

ELAINE. What do I have to do to be believed? Do I have to have videotape?

PETER. Actually, that's a good point. We do have videotape of each hotel room, just in case. But our judges have been reviewing the tape —

ELAINE. Thank god.

PETER. And from what they can tell, the tape corroborates … either version.

TOD. That's the thing. If he did what she says, then he'd have to make up a story *exactly* like the one he just …

PETER. *(Cutting him off.)* For now, it's up to our jury of peers. Guys? Who do you believe?

TONY, RACHEL, and TRACEY. Kent.

TOD. I mean — you know, what if — if she's not making this up …

PETER. *(Whisking away the blue dot.)* OK, sorry, Elaine. Better luck next time. Kent — you're back in the game and I just want you to know we're sorry your name got dragged through the mud. As long as women have the right to speak, well, what can we do?

KENT. I just want to put this behind me and get on with the game.

ELAINE. I didn't make it up.

PETER. Of course you didn't, honey. And no one's saying that. Maybe you fantasized it. Maybe you told him what to do. Maybe it was all a bad dream. But … time is ticking down, so let's hop on back to the others and go to our Final Moment of Ecstasy. *(Guests pull out blackboards, start scribbling.)* By now you've all gotten to know each other, and since we believe in romance on *The Morning After*, we'd like to think some of you will want to keep in touch, maybe make a go of it. Toward that end, each of you gets to pick who you'd like to go with on a dream vacation for two. If two of you pick each other, we'll foot the bill. Everyone just about done? *(Everyone has scribbled a name. They breast their blackboards. Elaine is a mess.)*

PETER. Tod.

TOD. Boy — you know, I just feel kind of bad about what happened.

PETER. Tod, relax, no one can even prove that anything happened worth feeling bad about. Why not just forget about it and tell us who you picked.

TOD. Well, Tracey and Elaine are great girls and I really like them and everything but I think … Rachel and I really found something beautiful and I'd like to take her with me to this beach I know in Mexico where the waves crash upon the moonlit shore and mushrooms are like, a dollar apiece.

PETER. Sounds bitch'n, Tod … Tony?

TONY. You know, I had a great time with Tracey, but then she's turned out to be a lying whore, like the other one, so I'd like to take *Rachel* to Vegas with me. First I'd show her off at the high roller table then spend the night in the room with her and some X-rated videos.

PETER. Don't get your hopes up, Tony. Kent — no hard feelings?

KENT. *(Reveals his blackboard.)* Only for Rachel. I found her intriguing and I'd really like to get to know her better. My family has a small compound off the Maryland coast and I'd like to bring her there for a quiet weekend.

PETER. OK. Rachel scores a hat trick. Tracey, you were shut out, but we'd like to know who you went for ...

TRACEY. Kent. He just seems like a real gentleman, and I wish he'd spent the night with me because I think he knows how to treat a lady. And I know how to treat a man. *(Looks at Tony.)* A real man.

PETER. Ouch, Tony. Tracey, a real pleasure having you with us. Elaine ... who's your lucky fella ... *(He reaches over and turns her blackboard for her. Scrawl.)* OK — no one caught your fancy. Maybe you'll come back some other time and have better luck. Rachel. Rachel. Rachel. All three of these guys like you, your personality, and those long lean legs of yours. Whichever guy you choose, you and he will get to go on his dream vacation ...

RACHEL. I just want to say this was the hardest decision I have ever had to make. All three of the guys are such ... fun. Tony — I wish we could have gotten to know each other, but I spent the night with Tod. Tod — it was a night I don't think I'll ever forget. Ever. And Peter, you've been really great too. So — I had a hard time choosing, but I just think that after what happened to Kent, he just handled himself so well. He seems so calm, and self-assured. Like Tracey said, a real gentleman. And very sexy. So — *(Turns her blackboard over.)* Kent ...

PETER. Yes! Rachel and Kent, you're our grand prize winners! Goodbye, everyone. See you tomorrow on *The Morning After.* *(He jumps up. Hugs her. Kisses her. Starts to get a little rough with her, for a second, then backs off. Meanwhile, Tod has given Tracey a hug. Tony waits to give Rachel a hug. Tod now also waits to give Rachel a hug. Elaine stays on the couch. Peter goes downstage and gives the home viewing audience a big kiss good night.)*

End of Play

PROPERTY LIST

Cup of coffee
Stick-on ribbons as prizes
Bouquet made of condoms
Card for host to read from
Large blue "dot" on a stick
Blackboards and chalk
Prize

SOUND EFFECTS

Wild sounds from audience: whoops, roars, applause, etc.
Bells ringing
Ding ding ding
Voices yelling STOP
Announcer voiceover

LOVE OF THE GAME

CHARACTERS

CAL BROMNELL — 35, successful MLB pitcher.

ASHLEY BROMNELL — 29, baseball wife. Attractive, well put-together.

JASON BROMNELL — Their son. Nine years old. Spoiled, good-looking kid.

LOVE OF THE GAME

Cal Bromnell, 35, successful MLB pitcher, does some shoulder rotations on his patio. He's focused. Doesn't even notice Ashley as she enters (Ashley, 29, baseball wife. She knows the cameras will go to her as her husband pitches, and she's ready. Make-up, jewelry, low-cut top).

ASHLEY. Is now a good time? *(He stops. Cold.)*
CAL. I'm pitching tonight. *(Picks up a ball, rotates it. Spins, curls his fingers around it. Tosses it to himself.)*
ASHLEY. Yesterday you said, you were "late for the ballpark. Could we talk later?" Then you said, "not at the stadium," so I didn't. Then you said you had to go out with the guys, then this morning you said you had to do your stretches … *(She intercepts the ball from him.)* So, is now a good time?
CAL. No. Now is the worst time. I'm pitching in three hours. Whatever it is you want to buy now, tell me about it tomorrow. *(He resumes stretching.)*
ASHLEY. I don't want to buy anything. I told you. It's about Jason. He got into a fight in school while you were on the road.
CAL. *(In mid-stretch.)* Did he win?
ASHLEY. How about, "Is he OK?"
CAL. If he won, he's OK.
ASHLEY. No he's not OK. If he were OK, the Summer School guidance counselor wouldn't be calling me in to discuss his problems.
CAL. Boys get into fights. That's what boys do. I'll get this guidance counselor some tickets, to the next homestand —
ASHLEY. He was fighting about you.
CAL. *(Proud.)* No kidding?
ASHLEY. This other kid, Caroline —
CAL. A girl. He hit a girl.
ASHLEY. She's pretty tough. She's half a foot taller than him, keeps her hair cut short, plays co-ed soccer —
CAL. Well, that's OK then.

ASHLEY. And she was teasing him about you —

CAL. *(Upset.)* Me? I've won three straight. I'm out of my slump, what's this kid's problem.

ASHLEY. It doesn't matter, Cal.

CAL. I just … I'm curious. What'd she say.

ASHLEY. *(Relents.)* It was about the beanball. She said your control was off, you hit Bradley by mistake —

CAL. *(Snorts.)* Yeah, right.

ASHLEY. That's what you told ESPN.

CAL. That's what you're supposed to say. Everyone knows that —

ASHLEY. Jason felt he had to protect your honor.

CAL. *(Beaming.)* No kidding?

ASHLEY. Cal. He's getting into trouble because he's got a temper, and he fights his way out of problems. He needs to know, from you — that that never works.

CAL. I've told him that … haven't I?

ASHLEY. You need to tell him the truth about the pitch —

CAL. Sounds like he gets it.

ASHLEY. No, Cal. He needs to hear, from you, that the pitch really did get away from you, that you would never throw at a batter. That —

CAL. Bradley's a punk. Crowds the box. Hits a home run and stands at the plate admiring his shot. That's bush league.

ASHLEY. And what is beaning him?

CAL. Hard ball. I strike someone out, maybe I make a quick pumping gesture. But I keep my head down. Go on to the next. Professional. An assassin shoots someone — he doesn't taunt his victim, he packs up and moves on. Bradley's a showboat. Real attitude. So I took the wind out of his sails. *(She stares at him. He can't stop himself now.)* Next inning … I come up to bat. Badge is catching for them. He whispers to me: "Next time, hit that prick so he don't get up." His own team-mates hate him, I — *(Finally realizes she's upset.)* What?

ASHLEY. Do you want your son to think you get even by decking someone instead of striking him out?

CAL. Well he struck out the next time.

ASHLEY. Cal — Jason has problems. The guidance counselor is concerned.

CAL. I told you, I'll talk to the guy, give him some tickets, straighten it out.

ASHLEY. It's a she, she doesn't know baseball, and who you

should talk to is Jason.

CAL. Aw Jesus. I got a game tonight … in three hours.

ASHLEY. And if you talk to him, on a game night, he'll realize how seriously you take this. *(He looks at her.)*

CAL. How about —

ASHLEY. *(Calls, into the house.)* Jason! Your father wants to talk to you. *(No response.)* Now! *(She kisses Cal. Tosses him back the ball she took from him. Cal watches her leave. Practices looking stern. Parental poses. Pointing his finger. Doesn't see Jason [nine, spoiled, good looking] enter, who watches him prepping to lecture.)*

JASON. Yo dad. Don't you have a game tonight?

CAL. Yes. Yes I do … son. But this is … important.

JASON. Can't it wait until —

CAL. No. I understand you got into a fight, with a girl, while I was away.

JASON. She's not really a girl girl, dad. She makes everyone call her Carl. And —

CAL. Doesn't matter. Girl or boy, you shouldn't go around hitting people.

JASON. She called you a woos.

CAL. She what. Well … OK I see why you got mad. She really said that?

JASON. Ah huh. Said that when you were in the AL, you brushed 'em back on purpose, but now in the NL, since there's no DH, and you have to bat, you're afraid of getting knocked down when you come to bat.

CAL. Oh, that's just crap.

JASON. That's why I had to defend you.

CAL. Jace, I can see why you got mad. And all. *(Looks off, senses, or sees, Ashley is watching.)* But you know what … you don't hit people for saying things that upset you.

JASON. She started it. I told her you knew what you were doing. That if you knocked someone on their … butt, you did it on purpose. Then she said you just don't have control anymore. So I knocked her on her butt and said, "Sorry, that must have been an accident too." *(Cal tries to hide his enjoyment of this. From offstage now:)*

ASHLEY. *(From offstage.)* Cal, you've got a game to go to.

CAL. *(Takes the hint.)* This Caroline, or Carl, or whatever her name is … She's … right. I just, the ball just got away from me.

JASON. C'mon dad. No way you —

CAL. I'm serious. The ball just got away from me. It happens.

113

(Jason is upset. His old man isn't as tough as he thought.) Hey — you should be proud of your old man. I don't need to bean someone to win. I just have to out-think him. You remember Game Five, ALCS. JASON. Bottom of the eighth, Two on, two out. Jeter — *(Jason now becomes Jeter, Cal becomes ... Cal. They reenact the at-bat.)*
CAL. — who's always good in the clutch —
JASON. *(Takes a practice swing.)* — at the plate. Two balls, one strike.
CAL. Three straight fast balls, inside. He's set up for the change, on the outside corner.
JASON. *(As Jeter: swing, misses.)* Strike two.
CAL. Now the curve. Down and in. See if he'll fish.
JASON. *("Taking" all the way.)* Ball. Full count.
CAL. He knows, he just knows, I have to come in with my heat. Down the pipe. So he steps in. I see it, and I throw the change low and in. He's handcuffed. So far out in front, he's swung and missed before the ball has crossed the plate.
JASON. Strike three. Inning over. And the crowd goes wild. Woo woo woo.
CAL. I didn't brush him back. I didn't even blow it by him. I out-thought him. That's how you win, Jason. With this. *(Points to his head.)* Not these. *(He points to his fists.)* Your old man is too good a pitcher to take a cheap shot. And you're too smart to get into trouble over nothing. OK? *(Jason nods. Depressed as hell. Cal now shadowboxes playfully with his kid. Ashley comes out, hands Cal a coffee thermos.)*
ASHLEY. You have a game to pitch Cal, you're going to be late.
CAL. *(Bad acting.)* Oh — that's OK, this was more important.
ASHLEY. So you two had a good talk?
JASON. *(Not giving her the satisfaction.)* Whatever. *(Ashley kisses Cal on the forehead.)*
ASHLEY. I'll back the Hummer out. *(Heads to the garage. Cal follows.)*
JASON. Dad — *(Cal stops, turns.)* Dad, if you could paint the corners on Jeter, no way hitting Bradley was an accident. *(Cal checks, sees Ashley is out of earshot.)*
CAL. Don't tell your mom. *(He winks. Tosses his son the ball. Walks offstage to the garage and his wife.)*

End of Play

PROPERTY LIST

Baseball

AMICI, ASCOLTATE

CHARACTERS

UNCLE GUY

TONY

ROSE

DOM

JOE

AMICI, ASCOLTATE

2007. Tony, mid-50s, in his Cleveland living room. Anxious. A couch and coffee table onstage with him. Upstage, a young extremely anxious Italo-American soldier, Uncle Guy, looks out at a sea of advancing Italian soldiers. Somewhere in Sicily. 1944.

UNCLE GUY. *(Shouting.) Amici, ascoltate!*
TONY. ... Listen, friends.
UNCLE GUY. *Amici, ascoltate.*
TONY. "Listen, friends," those were the two words my Uncle Guy said in World War Two. In Sicily. The only two words of Italian he could think of, the two words that saved his life and made him a war hero. *(Lights on a young Itala-American mother, Rose, who enters from the opposite side of the stage. She's a wreck. It's 1969.)*
ROSE. What's his number?
TONY. Those were the three words —
ROSE. What's his fucking number?
TONY. Or four, my mother said, as my father and I sat in this living room and watched the first nationally televised draft lottery. I was eighteen. Until that day, I had never had a gun pointed at me. And to this day, I've never shot one. *(Lights on Uncle Dom, Guy's "sissy" twin. He walks in pain, maybe uses a cane. [Note: Dom, Guy and later, Joey, should all be played by same actor.])*
DOM. The nurses held the Lucky Strikes to our lips, and the morphine dripped like morning dew.
TONY. That's Uncle Dom, Uncle Guy's ... "artistic" twin, talking about the long slow hospital boat that took him home from the Battle of Biche, in France.
DOM. *(To Tony.)* Bitch. The Battle of the Bitch, we called it.
TONY. Dom had been a bit of a ... sissy in the neighborhood.
DOM. *(To Tony.)* I was useless with a gun, I mean, I was studying fabric design before I enlisted. The army saw my resume, they figured if I could sew fabric I could sew skin so they took away my

119

gun, and made me a medic — the lowest of the low. No training, just scrubbed pots all night long in basic, while everyone called us girl names. Not too much later, we're storming the beaches of France. Blood was everywhere — rivers of it, for months. These poor beautiful boys would run, hell for leather, into a firestorm.

TONY. And if they got hit, you'd run right after them. To save them.

DOM. That was my job. And I didn't save them. They knew they we're dying, I knew they were dying. I just held them. And we'd laugh, and talk about the future.

TONY. *(To audience.)* Until the day Dom got hit. Blown fifty yards. Shrapnel in his back, shattering his pelvis. He never walked without pain, and he was was never able to have sex again. Something he told me, a week before he died. *(Tony looks to an off-stage room.)* He's sleeping now, but tomorrow morning my son goes to war, Iraq. And tonight, after too much grappa, I am thinking about him, and about my war hero uncles, and my father who landed on Iwo Jima. And my nonna, who had three sons at war, at the same time. *(Lights on Nonna [played by same actress who played Rose], an old-world Italian mother.)*

NONNA. *Non ho dormito, neanche una notte, per cinque anni.*

TONY. Their mother, my nonna, was already a widow when they left. She'd been here thirty years, and spoke maybe thirty words of English.

NONNA. *(To Tony.)* I no sleepa one night, neanche one night, for five years. If I sleep, the men with the telegram, they gonna come.

TONY. When Dom the last one back, arrived home, with his purple heart, and bronze star, his mother, my grandmother, fell to her knees. When she stopped crying, she said the sentence in English she'd been practicing the entire year he was in rehab.

NONA. Dominic, Your country isa proud of you.

DOM. Mama, they could care less. *(To Tony.)* When the Army told me, I'd never walk again, I knew I would. The Army is always wrong.

TONY. I know, Dom. *(Returns to audience.)* Tomorrow, my son goes to war, and tonight, I tell myself nonna got through worse, on her own. Her husband, my grandfather, Guiseppe, didn't make it through the depression. When I was forty, I went to the village he grew up in, and I found out, it's a miracle he got here at all.

My grandfather, Guiseppe, in an olive grove hidden by his father. The young men, or boys, of the village are being forcibly conscripted. It's 1912 and a few months earlier Italy had gone to war, against the Turks, in Libya. Now, the Libyans were known to hate the Turks, and it was understood they would greet the Italian Navy as liberators. It was going to be "una passegiatta": a military stroll. Within five weeks of the first attack, Italy claimed its suzerainty over Libya. Mission Accomplished. And then, Libyan rebels joined forces with the Turks, they encircled and decimated the ill-prepared Italian forces. Attempts to pacify the locals were met with resistance, and when the Italians responded with brutal repression, the rebels numbers grew. Twenty thousand Italian soldiers and sailors were initially sent to war, suddenly 80,000 more were needed. My grandfather Guiseppe, hid in the olive grove until nightfall, then made his way to the sea, and L'America.

He did not prosper here, but before he died from overwork and overdrink, he met my nonna and fathered three sons. When the Japanese bombed Pearl Harbor, the Marino boys, all three of them enlisted. The next day my father, the oldest, was sent to the Pacific Theater. He was an Italian-American, and the army thought boys like that would be a security risk in Sicily.

Uncle Guy, enlisted ten minutes later. He was sent to Europe. He was an Italian-American; and the army thought boys like that might be useful once the invasion of Sicily began. *(Lights on Uncle Guy.)*

UNCLE GUY. *(To Tony.)* Your father and I could never make sense of that one. I'm sent to Sicily, on one of the first boats. I figured, when we landed, I'd be used as a translator. Or maybe sent into the villages once we'd captured them. What the fuck did I know. When we land, my sergeant yells out "Where's the dago?" and tells me about my special assignment.

"Marino, climb that tree," he orders.

What for, I asked.

"We're leaving you behind, as a sniper. The Guineas know we've landed. You climb that tree. When they start to come up over the hill, you start to fire."

And then what, I asked.

"You just keep firing , until one of them takes you out."

I'm a good dumb soldier, so I climb the tree, and my company moves out. At dawn I hear noises, I turn and see 120 Italian soldiers climbing over the hill in back of me. Before I can take aim, they've seen me. I freeze. They freeze. I put my hands to my mouth, and I shout the only two friggen words of Italian I can think of, "amici ascoltate, amici ascoltate."

They are hungry, and tired. They know the war is over. The

whole regiment looks at me, looks to each other, they drop their guns to the ground. Hands in the air.

The first American they meet is a paisan, they figure they've stepped in shit and found gold. I march them into camp at gun point. *(Pointedly to Tony.)* My son Ritty, when he went to Vietnam, I told him, don't be the hero. Come back in one piece. Stupid sonofabitch … your mother, she was right. *(Lights down on Guy. Back on Tony.)*

TONY. Ritty, my cousin, Guy's son. Short order cook. He went over to Vietnam — the Marinos, we've never been good at deferments — in '68. *(Lights on Rose, upset. Pacing.)*

ROSE. Have you read these?

TONY. His letters from the Delta seem to be written by someone who has gone insane. *(Tony moves to the living room couch.)* December 1969. I am eighteen. Out of high school, single, without a thought about going to college. Which means, I am eligible for the draft. Only this year, they've decided to have a draft lottery. On TV. If your number is low, you are going to Vietnam, and you are going to die. We're in the living room, watching on a black and white Sylvania. I'm scared shitless, and this is before my mother tells me, she has a plan.

ROSE. *(Winking, to Tony.)* Don't worry. You're not going to fight the Viet Cong. *(Joey, Tony's father, enters the living room area.)*

JOEY. What do you mean, he's not going? If he's drafted, he's going.

TONY. *(To audience.)* My parents, who married ten days after they met, and since then, have agreed on nothing in their entire marriage, find themselves on opposite sides of the great debate. My father is perhaps the last Democrat in America who believes in the domino theory.

JOE. *(To Rose and Tony.)* If Vietnam falls, then we lose Cambodia, and Laos and Thailand. The Red Chinese march into South Korea, and Japan.

ROSE. Oh sure they do.

JOE. The Russians break through the Iron Curtain. You laugh at me, you won't laugh under communism.

ROSE. He's not going over there. I'm not going to be like your brother Guy, up all night worrying about Rittie. The poor stoonade's gone crazy in the head over there.

JOE. So you want your son to go to prison, Rosie?

ROSE. He won't have to. If his number's low, I'm going to shoot his fucking pinky off. They won't take him if he's missing a finger.

TONY. Ma.

JOE. Ro —

ROSE. What number are they up to?

JOE. Why don't we turn this off, we'll read about it — *(Joe starts to walk to the TV. Rose pulls a gun on him.)*

ROSE. Don't you fucking move. *(Joe stops.)*

JOE. Ro — where did you — Put that gun down. *(He starts toward her.)*

ROSE. Take one more step, one step and I'll shoot you in your fucking balls. *(She re-aims the gun at his groin.)*

TONY. My father who landed on Iwo Jima, and was fired upon by kamikazes, takes one look at my mother, and stops in his tracks.

ROSE. *(To Tony.)* And you, smart ass, put your left hand out on the table, where I can see it. *(Tony looks at her, puts his hand on the table. To Joe.)* It's only a pinky, what does he need it for?

TONY. So we watched the lottery together, at gunpoint. While little plastic capsules were pulled by hand out of a big glass jar. I still remember September fourteenth was number one. April twenty-fourth was number two. My birthday, was number 321. I was never called. *(To Rose.)* Ma, was it really loaded? *(She hands it to Tony.)*

ROSE. You bet your sweet ass it was. *(Rose leaves. Tony gingerly places the gun on the coffee table.)*

TONY. Cousin Rittie, he finally made it home, but he'd been sprayed so many times with agent orange, his liver and lungs were no good. The VA swore the exposure had nothing to do with his problems. He died of liver cancer at thirty-three.

When Rittie died, we all went to the funeral. My father stood next to his brother Guy. They didn't say a word to each other. On the drive home, my father cries for the second time in his life.

JOE. It's unnatural, for a father to bury his son. That day, when your number came up, and I knew you weren't going to go, I went to move the car, and I broke down in tears. Don't tell your mother.

TONY. Dad, did you ever think about Nonna, alone, with the three boys overseas.

JOE. That was different. Everybody went. No one had it easy.

TONY. My father never talked much about … the War. When he did, he talked about the guys. The comraderie. Sergeant Nick, from Chicago, Dave "the Pollack" from Pennsylvania. Uncle Dom told me dad saw a lot of action. He was part of an anti-aircraft battery on one of the first ships to land at Iwo Jima. The Japanese knew the invasion was coming, so they sent kamikaze planes to hit the U.S.

ships. On the way in, they sunk the ship in front of him, and the ship behind him. He went below and prayed from a Pocket Bible. When they landed, they had to set up right away to take out the kamikazes. Guys were dropping like flies.

   After my father died, I found a trunk in the attic. The Pocket Bible was there. And also, a stack of letters he'd written to Nonna, with a rubber band around them.

JOE. *"Tutto va bene, mama. Non ti preoccupare. Tutto va bene."*

TONY. Everything is good, mama. Don't you worry. *(Joe leaves. Tony, alone onstage, looks to the offstage room.)* Somehow, all three Marino boys made it home. And Rittie didn't make it, and I didn't have to go. And now my son Joey, who went ROTC to pay for college, is sleeping, and in a few days he'll land in Iraq. And he'll write me emails, "don't worry, pops. I'm in the green zone. It's very safe here. Don't you worry"

It's almost dawn. Time to wake Joey up, and drive him to the airport. *(Tony starts toward the room, stops, returns to the coffee table at center stage. Picks up the gun his mother handed him.)* It's only a pinky. *(He resumes his walk to his son's room. Stops one last time, then continues.)*

End of Play

PROPERTY LIST

Gun

NEW PLAYS

★ **THE GREAT AMERICAN TRAILER PARK MUSICAL music and lyrics by David Nehls, book by Betsy Kelso.** Pippi, a stripper on the run, has just moved into Armadillo Acres, wreaking havoc among the tenants of Florida's most exclusive trailer park. "Adultery, strippers, murderous ex-boyfriends, Costco and the Ice Capades. Undeniable fun." *–NY Post.* "Joyful and unashamedly vulgar." *–The New Yorker.* "Sparkles with treasure." *–New York Sun.* [2M, 5W] ISBN: 978-0-8222-2137-1

★ **MATCH by Stephen Belber.** When a young Seattle couple meet a prominent New York choreographer, they are led on a fraught journey that will change their lives forever. "Uproariously funny, deeply moving, enthralling theatre." *–NY Daily News.* "Prolific laughs and ear-to-ear smiles." *–NY Magazine.* [2M, 1W] ISBN: 978-0-8222-2020-6

★ **MR. MARMALADE by Noah Haidle.** Four-year-old Lucy's imaginary friend, Mr. Marmalade, doesn't have much time for her—not to mention he has a cocaine addiction and a penchant for pornography. "Alternately hilarious and heartbreaking." *–The New Yorker.* "A mature and accomplished play." *–LA Times.* "Scathingly observant comedy." *–Miami Herald.* [4M, 2W] ISBN: 978-0-8222-2142-5

★ **MOONLIGHT AND MAGNOLIAS by Ron Hutchinson.** Three men cloister themselves as they work tirelessly to reshape a screenplay that's just not working—*Gone with the Wind.* "Consumers of vintage Hollywood insider stories will eat up Hutchinson's diverting conjecture." *–Variety.* "A lot of fun." *–NY Post.* "A Hollywood dream-factory farce." *–Chicago Sun-Times.* [3M, 1W] ISBN: 978-0-8222-2084-8

★ **THE LEARNED LADIES OF PARK AVENUE by David Grimm, translated and freely adapted from Molière's *Les Femmes Savantes.*** Dicky wants to marry Betty, but her mother's plan is for Betty to wed a most pompous man. "A brave, brainy and barmy revision." *–Hartford Courant.* "A rare but welcome bird in contemporary theatre." *–New Haven Register.* "Roll over Cole Porter." *–Boston Globe.* [5M, 5W] ISBN: 978-0-8222-2135-7

★ **REGRETS ONLY by Paul Rudnick.** A sparkling comedy of Manhattan manners that explores the latest topics in marriage, friendships and squandered riches. "One of the funniest quip-meisters on the planet." *–NY Times.* "Precious moments of hilarity. Devastatingly accurate political and social satire." *–BackStage.* "Great fun." *–CurtainUp.* [3M, 3W] ISBN: 978-0-8222-2223-1

DRAMATISTS PLAY SERVICE, INC.
440 Park Avenue South, New York, NY 10016   212-683-8960   Fax 212-213-1539
postmaster@dramatists.com   www.dramatists.com

NEW PLAYS

★ **AFTER ASHLEY by Gina Gionfriddo.** A teenager is unwillingly thrust into the national spotlight when a family tragedy becomes talk-show fodder. "A work that virtually any audience would find accessible." *–NY Times.* "Deft character-ization and caustic humor." *–NY Sun.* "A smart satirical drama." *–Variety.* [4M, 2W] ISBN: 978-0-8222-2099-2

★ **THE RUBY SUNRISE by Rinne Groff.** Twenty-five years after Ruby struggles to realize her dream of inventing the first television, her daughter faces similar battles of faith as she works to get Ruby's story told on network TV. "Measured and intelligent, optimistic yet clear-eyed." *–NY Magazine.* "Maintains an exciting sense of ingenuity." *–Village Voice.* "Sinuous theatrical flair." *–Broadway.com.* [3M, 4W] ISBN: 978-0-8222-2140-1

★ **MY NAME IS RACHEL CORRIE taken from the writings of Rachel Corrie, edited by Alan Rickman and Katharine Viner.** This solo piece tells the story of Rachel Corrie who was killed in Gaza by an Israeli bulldozer set to demol-ish a Palestinian home. "Heartbreaking urgency. An invigoratingly detailed por-trait of a passionate idealist." *–NY Times.* "Deeply authentically human." *–USA Today.* "A stunning dramatization." *–CurtainUp.* [1W] ISBN: 978-0-8222-2222-4

★ **ALMOST, MAINE by John Cariani.** This charming midwinter night's dream of a play turns romantic clichés on their ear as it chronicles the painfully hilarious amorous adventures (and misadventures) of residents of a remote northern town that doesn't quite exist. "A whimsical approach to the joys and perils of romance." *–NY Times.* "Sweet, poignant and witty." *–NY Daily News.* "Aims for the heart by way of the funny bone." *–Star-Ledger.* [2M, 2W] ISBN: 978-0-8222-2156-2

★ **Mitch Albom's TUESDAYS WITH MORRIE by Jeffrey Hatcher and Mitch Albom, based on the book by Mitch Albom.** The true story of Brandeis University professor Morrie Schwartz and his relationship with his stu-dent Mitch Albom. "A touching, life-affirming, deeply emotional drama." *–NY Daily News.* "You'll laugh. You'll cry." *–Variety.* "Moving and powerful." *–NY Post.* [2M] ISBN: 978-0-8222-2188-3

★ **DOG SEES GOD: CONFESSIONS OF A TEENAGE BLOCKHEAD by Bert V. Royal.** An abused pianist and a pyromaniac ex-girlfriend contribute to the teen-angst of America's most hapless kid. "A welcome antidote to the notion that the *Peanuts* gang provides merely American cuteness." *–NY Times.* "Hysterically funny." *–NY Post.* "The *Peanuts* kids have finally come out of their shells." *–Time Out.* [4M, 4W] ISBN: 978-0-8222-2152-4

DRAMATISTS PLAY SERVICE, INC.
440 Park Avenue South, New York, NY 10016 212-683-8960 Fax 212-213-1539
postmaster@dramatists.com www.dramatists.com

NEW PLAYS

★ **RABBIT HOLE by David Lindsay-Abaire.** Winner of the 2007 Pulitzer Prize. Becca and Howie Corbett have everything a couple could want until a life-shattering accident turns their world upside down. "An intensely emotional examination of grief, laced with wit." *—Variety.* "A transcendent and deeply affecting new play." *—Entertainment Weekly.* "Painstakingly beautiful." *—BackStage.* [2M, 3W] ISBN: 978-0-8222-2154-8

★ **DOUBT, A Parable by John Patrick Shanley.** Winner of the 2005 Pulitzer Prize and Tony Award. Sister Aloysius, a Bronx school principal, takes matters into her own hands when she suspects the young Father Flynn of improper relations with one of the male students. "All the elements come invigoratingly together like clockwork." *—Variety.* "Passionate, exquisite, important, engrossing." *—NY Newsday.* [1M, 3W] ISBN: 978-0-8222-2219-4

★ **THE PILLOWMAN by Martin McDonagh.** In an unnamed totalitarian state, an author of horrific children's stories discovers that someone has been making his stories come true. "A blindingly bright black comedy." *—NY Times.* "McDonagh's least forgiving, bravest play." *—Variety.* "Thoroughly startling and genuinely intimidating." *—Chicago Tribune.* [4M, 5 bit parts (2M, 1W, 1 boy, 1 girl)] ISBN: 978-0-8222-2100-5

★ **GREY GARDENS book by Doug Wright, music by Scott Frankel, lyrics by Michael Korie.** The hilarious and heartbreaking story of Big Edie and Little Edie Bouvier Beale, the eccentric aunt and cousin of Jacqueline Kennedy Onassis, once bright names on the social register who became East Hampton's most notorious recluses. "An experience no passionate theatergoer should miss." *—NY Times.* "A unique and unmissable musical." *—Rolling Stone.* [4M, 3W, 2 girls] ISBN: 978-0-8222-2181-4

★ **THE LITTLE DOG LAUGHED by Douglas Carter Beane.** Mitchell Green could make it big as the hot new leading man in Hollywood if Diane, his agent, could just keep him in the closet. "Devastatingly funny." *—NY Times.* "An out-and-out delight." *—NY Daily News.* "Full of wit and wisdom." *—NY Post.* [2M, 2W] ISBN: 978-0-8222-2226-2

★ **SHINING CITY by Conor McPherson.** A guilt-ridden man reaches out to a therapist after seeing the ghost of his recently deceased wife. "Haunting, inspired and glorious." *—NY Times.* "Simply breathtaking and astonishing." *—Time Out.* "A thoughtful, artful, absorbing new drama." *—Star-Ledger.* [3M, 1W] ISBN: 978-0-8222-2187-6

DRAMATISTS PLAY SERVICE, INC.
440 Park Avenue South, New York, NY 10016 212-683-8960 Fax 212-213-1539
postmaster@dramatists.com www.dramatists.com